THE ROMAN PRIMACY

TO A.D. 461

THE
ROMAN PRIMACY

TO A.D. 461

BY

B. J. KIDD, D.D.

WARDEN OF KEBLE COLLEGE, OXFORD; HON. CANON OF
CHRIST CHURCH; AND EXAMINING CHAPLAIN TO THE
BISHOPS OF LONDON AND OXFORD

*A PUBLICATION OF THE LITERATURE
ASSOCIATION OF THE CHURCH UNION*

WIPF & STOCK · Eugene, Oregon

Wipf and Stock Publishers
199 W 8th Ave, Suite 3
Eugene, OR 97401

The Roman Primacy to A. D. 461
By Kidd, B. J.
Copyright©1936 SPCK
ISBN 13: 978-1-60899-722-0
Publication date 6/16/2010
Previously published by SPCK, 1936

This Edition reprinted by Wipf and Stock Publishers
by arrangement with SPCK, London.

PREFATORY NOTE

Dom CUTHBERT BUTLER, in his *Vatican Council* (ii. 71), observes: " Though at the time of the Council it was the infallibility that raised the greatest storms . . . I cannot help thinking that the matter of the primacy, as defined in the third chapter of the dogmatic Constitution of July 18, in reality presents . . . much greater obstacles to that united Christendom in communion with the Apostolic See of Rome and its Bishop that is in our day increasingly the dream and the object of prayers and of strivings of countless men of goodwill still outside that communion." I think so too. We never got face to face with the question of a primacy of jurisdiction at Malines. But it has been constantly in my mind ever since. And hence this enquiry: where I have endeavoured to keep to the purely historical aspect of the question. I should like to thank my friend Dr. Stone for reading my MS.; and the Delegates of the Clarendon Press for allowing me to make use of my *History of the Church to A.D.* 461, which they published in 1922.

B. J. K.

CONTENTS

CHAPTER   PAGE

I. THE ROMAN CHURCH: C. 100-180   -   -   11

§ 1. THE FIRST EPISTLE OF CLEMENT TO THE CORIN-
THIANS   -   -   -   -   -   11

§ 2. THE EPISTLE OF IGNATIUS TO THE ROMANS   -   12

§ 3. ST. PETER AND ST. PAUL   -   -   -   14

§ 4. IRENÆUS   -   -   -   -   -   15

§ 5. THE EPISCOPAL LISTS -   -   -   -   16

II. THE ROMAN SEE: C. 200   -   -   -   20

III. CYPRIAN AND STEPHEN: C. 250 -   -   -   23

§ 1. CYPRIAN, BISHOP OF CARTHAGE, 248-†58   -   23

§ 2. THE CHARTER OF THE EPISCOPATE   -   -   24

§ 3. CATHEDRA PETRI   -   -   -   -   28

§ 4. SPAIN: BASILIDES AND MARTIALIS   -   -   29

§ 5. GAUL: MARCIAN, BISHOP OF ARLES   -   -   30

§ 6. TU ES PETRUS -   -   -   -   -   31

§ 7. FIRMILIAN, BISHOP OF CÆSAREA IN CAPPADOCIA,
232-†72   -   -   -   -   -   35

IV. ALEXANDRIA AND ANTIOCH   -   -   38

§ 1. DIONYSIUS, BISHOP OF ALEXANDRIA, 247-†65 -   38

§ 2. PAUL OF SAMOSATA, BISHOP OF ANTIOCH, C.
260-70   -   -   -   -   -   40

V. CONSTANTINE AND HIS SONS, 313-61   -   42

§ 1. DONATISM   -   -   -   -   -   42

§ 2. ARIANISM   -   -   -   -   -   45

§ 3. THE COUNCIL OF SARDICA, 343   -   -   46

§ 4. LIBERIUS, 352-†66   -   -   -   -   53

CHAPTER   PAGE

VI. DAMASUS, 366-†84   -   -   -   -   56

§ 1. THE WEALTH OF THE ROMAN SEE   -   56

§ 2. THE RESCRIPT OF GRATIAN   -   -   57

§ 3. BASIL, ARCHBISHOP OF CÆSAREA IN CAPPADOCIA, 370-†9   -   -   -   -   60

§ 4. THE COUNCIL OF CONSTANTINOPLE, 381   -   62

§ 5. AMBROSE AND THEODOSIUS   -   -   66

§ 6. THE FIRST OFFICIAL DEFINITION OF THE ROMAN CLAIMS, 382 -   -   -   -   68

VII. ROME AND AFRICA   -   -   -   -   73

§ 1. SIRICIUS, 384-†99   -   -   -   73

§ 2. INNOCENT I, 402-†17   -   -   77

§ 3. AFRICA: ROMA LOCUTA EST   -   -   81

§ 4. ST. JOHN CHRYSOSTOM, ARCHBISHOP OF CONSTANTINOPLE, 398-†407 -   -   -   85

§ 5. ZOSIMUS, 417-†8   -   -   -   87

§ 6. BONIFACE I, 418-†22 -   -   -   91

§ 7. CŒLESTINE I, 422-†32 -   -   -   95

§ 8. APIARIUS   -   -   -   -   97

VIII. THE COUNCIL OF EPHESUS, 431 -   -   106

§ 1. CŒLESTINE AND CYRIL   -   -   106

§ 2. THE FIRST SESSION, 22ND JUNE   -   108

§ 3. THE ROMAN LEGATES -   -   -   109

§ 4. THE EASTERN VIEW OF THE ROMAN CLAIMS -   111

§ 5. SIXTUS III, 432-†40 -   -   -   112

IX. ST. LEO THE GREAT: 440-†61 -   -   117

§ 1. HIS CONCEPTION OF THE ROMAN PRIMACY -   117

§ 2. ITS RECEPTION IN ITALY, SPAIN AND AFRICA -   123

§ 3. HILARY, ARCHBISHOP OF ARLES, 429-†49 -   124

§ 4. THE LATROCINIUM, 449   -   -   129

CONTENTS

PAGE

§ 5. APPEALS TO ROME : FLAVIAN, EUSEBIUS, THEODORET - - - - - 134

§ 6. PULCHERIA, 450-†3, AND MARCIAN, 450-†7 - 137

§ 7. THE COUNCIL OF CHALCEDON, 451 - - 140

§ 8. THE FOURTH SESSION, 17TH OCT.: THE COUNCIL AND THE TOME - - - - 143

§ 9. THE TWENTY-EIGHTH CANON - - 144

§ 10. A VICTORY FOR THE FAITH - - - 147

§ 11. PRIMACY AND JURISDICTION - - - 152

INDEX - - - - - 156

CHAPTER I

THE ROMAN CHURCH

THE Roman primacy means the authority enjoyed at first by the local church of Rome and then by its bishop. It is everywhere recognized: but, in the case of the bishop, it may mean anything from a " primacy of honour "[1] to a primacy involving " full and supreme power of jurisdiction over the whole Church."[2]

At first, the primacy was that of the local Roman church. It had an acknowledged pre-eminence among other churches.

§ 1. This is evident, first, from *the Epistle of Clement to the Corinthians*,[3] written about A.D. 96. At Corinth, some members of the church had risen up against their clergy,[4] and had deposed them from office.[5] News of this reached Rome.[6] The Roman church, without being asked,[7] intervened on its own authority; and sent a letter, written by Clement, but in the name of the church,[8] reprimanding the Corinthians for such behaviour. St. John the Apostle was still alive; and

---

[1] Council of Constantinople, 381, c. 3: see W. Bright, *Notes on the Canons of the First Four General Councils, ad loc.*

[2] Vatican Council, 1870; *Const. dogm. I de eccl. Christi,* c. 3: *ap.* C. Mirbt⁴, *Quellen zur Geschichte des Papsttums,* No. 606.

[3] J. B. Lightfoot, *The Apostolic Fathers,* 5-40: extracts in Mirbt⁴, Nos. 5-7.

[4] 1 Clem. *ad Cor.* xlvii. § 6.

[5] *Ib.* xliv. §§ 4-6.   [6] *Ib.* xlvii. § 7.

[7] παρ' ὑμῖν not παρ' ὑμῶν: *Ib.* i. c. 1.   [8] *Ib.*: Salutation.

it is sometimes said that, this being so, the authority
thus exercised from Rome was clearly greater than
that of an Apostle other than St. Peter. But intervention came from Rome rather than from Ephesus,
simply because relations between Corinth and Rome
were more intimate than between Corinth and Ephesus.[1]
Nevertheless, the authority thus exercised by the
Roman church points to a primacy then no sooner
exercised than admitted. " The Roman church, by
the mouthpiece of Clement, intervened with imposing
authority";[2] and Clement's letter, as we learn from
the correspondence of Dionysius, bishop of Corinth,
c. 170, was still read in church there a generation later.[3]

§ 2. *The Epistle* of St. Ignatius *to the Romans*,[4]
written c. 110-7, equally testifies to the prestige of the
Roman church. " He is a staunch advocate of epis-
copacy "; yet in this letter to the church of Rome there
is not " the faintest allusion to the episcopal office
from first to last." It is the community to which he
appeals: " not to intercede and thus by obtaining
a pardon or commutation of sentence to rob him of
the crown of martyrdom."[5] Such is their influence,
he seems to assume, with the government. But not
less, in his view, is the primacy of the Roman church
among other churches. The church is addressed,

---

[1] See " L'intervention de l'Église de Rome à Corinthe
vers l'an 96." By R. van Caulewaert, in *Revue d'Hist. Eccl.*
for April 1935.

[2] L. Duchesne, *Christian Worship*[5], 15.

[3] Eus., *H. E.* IV. xxiii. 11.: Mirbt[4], No. 34: *Doc. Ch. Hist*
i., No. 54

[4] Lightfoot, *Ap. Fathers*, 119-23: Mirbt[4], No. 8.

[5] Lightfoot, *Clement* i. 71.

in the opening salutation, as " she who hath the presidency in the place of the region of the Romans."[1] But it is a " presidency of love,"[2] and this, according to Ignatius, was " the original primacy of Rome, a primacy not of official authority but of practical goodness, backed, however, by the prestige and the advantages which were necessarily enjoyed by the church of the metropolis." To this " moral ascendancy of the early Roman church, which was the historical foundation of its primacy,"[3] there is further testimony from Dionysius, bishop of Corinth. " This," he writes to Soter, bishop of Rome 175-182, " hath been your

---

[1] Ἐκκλησία . . . ἥτις καὶ προκάθηται ἐν τόπῳ χωρίου Ῥωμαίων [Mirbt⁴, No. 8]: presides [takes the precedence] either (1) in the country or district of the Romans or (2) describing not the range of the supremacy but the locality of the supreme power itself. " In this case, προκάθηται would be used absolutely of a certain precedency assigned to the church " (in any case, not the see) of Rome, " as situated in the Metropolis of the Empire and the world, over the other churches of Christendom. But if so, why ἐν τόπῳ χωρίου P. in place of ἐν Ῥώμῃ, which alone would be natural to describe merely the locality ?" Lightfoot, ad loc. (Ap. Fathers, II. i. 190 sq). Duchesne, however, argues in favour of the meaning that " l'église romaine préside á l'ensemble des églises." Les églises séparées, 127 sqq.

[2] προκαθημένη τῆς ἀγάπης, according to Funk, is only intelligible in connexion with a place or a collectivity, e.g. προκ. τῆς ἀνατόλης or προκ. τῆς οἰκουμένης: Ἀγάπη describes a collectivity, not a virtue, in this connexion, i.e.= " church," as in ἀγάπη Σμυρναίων καὶ Ἐφεσίων (Trall. xiii. 1); ἡ ἀγάπη τῶν ἐκκλησίων (Rom. ix. 3); ἡ ἀγάπη τῶν ἀδελφῶν τῶν ἐν Τρωάδι (Philad. xi. 2). " Puis donc qu'une église locale peut être appelée ἀγάπη, pourquoi ce même mot ne designerait-il pas l'église universelle ? Tel est l'argument de M. Funk—argument qui pose un possibilité plutôt qu'une conclusion."—P. Batiffol L'église naissante⁵, 169.

[3] Lightfoot, Clement i. 70.

practice from the beginning: to do good to all the brethren in various ways and to send supplies to many churches in every city."[1]

§ 3. There is, however, another element recognised by both Clement and Ignatius, as contributing to the pre-eminence of the church of Rome: its connexion with the Apostles Peter and Paul. It is probable that they both were martyred in the Neronian persecution about the year 64. Clement seems to have known them personally: for he speaks of them as " the good apostles "[2] and ranks them among those who had suffered under Nero: while Ignatius refers to them as having exercised authority in Rome. " I do not enjoin you," he says, " as Peter and Paul did. They were apostles: I am a convict."[3] Besides the prestige of its own charity and of its being the church of the capital, the Roman church from the first enjoyed the pre-eminence if not of apostolic origin[4] (for its origin was fortuitous) at any rate of apostolic organisation. It is in this sense that Irenæus, c. 185, speaks of it in the well-known passage, as " the most great and ancient and universally known church, founded and established at Rome by the two most glorious apostles Peter and Paul."[5]

[1] Eus., *H.E.* IV. xxiii. 10: Mirbt[4] No. 34: *Doc. Ch. Hist.* i., No. 54.

[2] 1 Clem. *ad Cor.* v. § 3: Mirbt[4], No. 5: *Doc. Ch. Hist.* i., No. 11.

[3] *Ep. ad Rom.* iv. § 3: Mirbt[4], No. 8.

[4] On the " fortuitous " origin of the Roman church, see Sanday and Headlam, *Romans*, pp. xxv-xxxi.

[5] *Adv. Hær.* III. iii. § 1: Mirbt[4], No. 40: *Doc. Ch. Hist.* i., No. 74.

§ 4. Irenæus continues: " *Ad* hanc enim ecclesiam propter potiorem [v.l. potentiorem] principalitatem *necesse est* omnem *convenire* ecclesiam, hoc est, eos qui sunt undique fideles, *in qua* semper ab his qui sunt undique conservata est ea quæ est ab apostolis traditio."[1] This is usually translated: " With this church because of its more influential pre-eminence it is necessary that every church should agree," so that communion with the Roman church is thus made the test of being in possession of the Christian truth. But the Latin will not bear this meaning, for (1) *necesse est* means " must " not " ought " which would require *oportet* and (2) *convenire ad* means not " agree with " but " resort to," while (3) " the apostolic tradition as to truth is preserved there " (*in qua* = the Roman church) by " those of the faithful " who " resort thither " for business or pleasure, and bring it with them rather than find it there. It is thus because the Roman church is Christendom in miniature that truth may best be found there; and hence from the consentient testimony of the various churches,[2] which finds constant witness at Rome, the pre-eminent authority of the Roman church. Add to this its apostolic " founders," and we have a further reason for its prestige. By the end of the second century Caius, a presbyter of Rome, points to the " trophies " of the two Apostles as existing in his day on the Vatican and by the Ostian Way.[3]

---

[1] *Adv. Hær.* III. iii. § 2.

[2] For an expansion of this argument see Tertullian, *De præscr. hær.* § 36: Mirbt[4], No. 51.

[3] Eus., *H. E.* II. xxv. 6, 7.: Mirbt[4], No. 45: *Doc. Ch. Hist.* i., No. 53.

This is conclusive evidence as to the belief of the Roman church at that date. Dead, as formerly when alive, their Apostolic founders were still among them.

§ 5. A further point arises from the connexion of this Apostolic " foundation " with the episcopate which in Rome succeeded it. There are four lists[1] of the early succession of bishops of Rome which have come down to us. They are those of (1) Hegesippus,[2] *c.* 160, preserved in full by Epiphanius,[3] *c.* 375; (2) Irenæus, who, continuing the passage quoted above, says: " The blessed Apostles, having founded and established the church [in Rome], entrusted the office of the episcopate to Linus . . . Anencletus succeeded him and, after Anencletus, in the third place from the Apostles, Clement received the episcopate . . . "[4] The third list (3) is that which lay before Eusebius and was utilized by him for his *History*,[5] 323 and his *Chronicle*,[6] 325. It is reconstructed for us by Lightfoot. These three lists have points in common. All three are of Eastern *provenance*, preserved as they are by Hegesippus, Irenæus and Eusebius: writers connected with the East. All rank the Apostles, Peter and Paul, in a class by themselves. All reckon the bishops of Rome in a succession that begins after the Apostolic

---

[1] Lightfoot, *Clement* i. 63 sq. (summary) and 201 sqq. (detailed).

[2] Eus., *H. E.* IV. xxii. 3: Mirbt[4], No. 30: *Doc. Ch. Hist.* i., No. 63.

[3] *Hær.* xxvii. § 6.

[4] *Adv. Hær.* III. iii. 3: Mirbt[4], No. 41.

[5] References in Lightfoot, *Clement* i. 206 sq.

[6] *Ib.* 207 sq.

founders of their church.[1]   And in all, the order of the
first three bishops of Rome is Linus, Cletus [Anencle-
tus], Clement.   It is thus the order traditional by the
middle of the second century.   But (4) a fourth list
presents considerable divergences.   It consists of a
catalogue of Roman bishops which forms one of several
tracts collected and edited in Rome A.D. 354 under
Pope Liberius.   This *Liberian Catalogue*[2] is a Western
list, as emanating from the local church in Rome; and
it ranks Peter as the first bishop of Rome.   It is attri-
butable to Hippolytus,[3] the scholar-bishop in Rome
†c. 236, though Hippolytus is not to be credited with
its blunders[4] in putting Clement second to Linus.
The editor of the *Catalogue* was, perhaps, not blunder-
ing but blending.   He had a definite intention—to
blend " two earlier traditions, the true (as above) which
places Clement third and the false which places him
first; the divergence being compromised, after the
manner of compromises, by placing him second."[5]
Thus, as an authoritative record, the Western, or
Liberian Catalogue of the Roman succession must give
way to the Eastern reckoning.   And this original form
of the tradition occupies a position of unique authority

  [1] In these lists, Hyginus is eighth after the Apostles: but
in other places Irenæus calls him " ninth " (*Adv. Hær.* I.
xxvii. 1; III. iv. 3) and therefore implies, so it is said, that
Peter was the first, and thus included in the list of the bishops
of Rome.   But the Latin has " octavus " and the Greek
ἔννατος is a mistake: see A. Stieren *ad loc.*, and E. Denny,
Papalism, §§ 476-7.
  [2] Lightfoot, *Clement* i. 64 and 253 sqq.; Mirbt[4], No. 125.
  [3] Lightfoot, i. 261.
  [4] *Ib.* 275.
  [5] C. H. Turner, *Studies in Early Church History*, 160.

among the churches of the Roman obedience to-day;
for the *Canon of the Mass*, after commemorating " Thy
blessed apostles and martyrs Peter and Paul " and the
other apostles goes on to mention, as in another division,
" Linus, Cletus, Clement," in a paragraph[1] which
probably belongs to the days of Pope Symmachus,
498-†514.

Important conclusions follow from these episcopal
lists. First, the Roman church was " founded " by
the two chief Apostles. Second, it was governed from
apostolic times by a continuous succession of bishops,
of whom the first was not St. Peter, but Linus. And it
is this apostolic foundation, coupled with the greatness
of the city, the consequent wealth and charity of its
church, and the orthodoxy, or tradition of truth, so
constantly reinforced there by the stream of visitors
from other churches, that rightly gave to the Roman
church its unique pre-eminence at that early date.
At no point in its history is this pre-eminence so evident
as under Pope Victor, 189-†98: when " from Gaul to
Osrhœne[2] [on the Euphrates]" his invitation[3] for the
summoning of councils to effect a settlement of the
Paschal Controversy was everywhere accepted. " This
initiative of Pope Victor alone, an initiative proved
to be effective, suffices to show how evident in those
ancient times was the exceptional situation and the

---

[1] *Communicantes :* and, on its date, see Batiffol, *Leçons sur la Messe*, 228.

[2] Eus., *H. E.* V. xxiii. 3: Mirbt[4], No. 35.

[3] *Ib.* xxiv. 8: Letter of Polycrates, bishop of Ephesus, to Pope Victor: Mirbt[4], No. 35: *Doc. Ch. Hist.* i. No. 82.

œcumenical authority of the Roman church."[1]   Yet
" the power of the bishop of Rome was built upon the
power of the church of Rome.   It was originally a
primacy, not of the episcopate, but of the church."[2]

[1] L. Duchesne, *The Churches separated from Rome*, 95.
[2] Lightfoot, *Clement* i. 70.

CHAPTER II

THE ROMAN SEE

WITH the opening of the third century, appear the foundations of " the later Roman theory that the Church of Rome derives all its authority from the bishop of Rome as the successor of St. Peter."[1] This is the second stage in the development of the Roman Primacy: and we now have to see how it came about.

Tertullian, writing about A.D. 198, the last year of Pope Victor, develops the argument from tradition taken over from Irenæus, as follows: " If there be any heresies which venture to plant themselves in the midst of the age of the Apostles . . . let them make known the origins of their churches, let them unfold the roll of their bishops, so coming down in succession from the beginning that their first bishop had for his ordainer and predecessor some one of the apostles, or of apostolic men, so he were one that continued steadfast with the apostles. For in this manner do the apostolic churches reckon their origin; as the church of Smyrna recounteth that Polycarp was placed there by John; as that of Rome doth, that Clement was placed there by Peter."[2] Here we find noted a tendency to go back, in proof of the claim to apostolicity, to some single apostolic founder, and to reckon him as the

[1] Lightfoot, *Clement* i. 70.
[2] Tert., *De præscr. hær.* c. xxxii, Mirbt[4], No. 52.

first bishop; and, if it be asked whence did Tertullian get the information that the church of Rome had an apostle for its first founder and consecrator of his successor as bishop, an answer may be found in the spurious *Epistle of Clement to James*,[1] " the date " of which " can hardly be earlier than the middle of the second century or much later than the beginning of the third."[2] The letter belonged to the Clementine Romances, of various date, which had such a vogue because of the name of Clement; and would thus be nowhere more popular than in Rome itself. Peter is here represented, shortly before his death, as " laying hands upon Clement as bishop of the Romans and entrusting to him his chair of discourse." It is true enough, as is clear from both the literary and the archæological evidence of this date, that Peter and Paul—sometimes Paul and Peter[3]—were still venerated as the co-founders of the Roman church. Its " earliest documents and traditions bear constant reference to Peter and Paul; never, before the third century, is the name of the one mentioned without corresponding mention of the other."[4] But it is also true that, from this time forward, Paul began to drop out and Peter to come into sole prominence as first bishop of Rome with Clement for his immediate accessor. For it is now that the Irenæan method of reckoning Peter and

[1] Mirbt[4], No. 85: *Doc. Ch. Hist.* i., No. 86.

[2] Lightfoot, *Clement* i. 414.

[3] See the inscriptions (*graffiti*) in *Saint Sébastien hors les Murs* (Paris, 1925), p. 58, with photographs, pp. 76 sq.: preface by Mgr. Batiffol. They are of the third century: *ib.*, p. 61.

[4] C. H. Turner, *Catholic and Apostolic*, 219.

Paul in one class as apostles and Linus and his successors in another class as bishops began to give way; and a new mode of reckoning came in about A.D. 220. Both Callistus, 217-†22, and his rival Hippolytus adopt it; counting Peter first bishop of Rome, and the latter referring to Pope Victor as the thirteenth bishop of Rome from Peter.[1] Significant too, and natural enough at this date, is the first appearance of the Petrine text (Mt. xvi. 18, 19) in connexion with the Roman See. For Pope Callistus claimed to derive his authority simply from Peter. It was not, however, any papal authority that he claimed, but only the power of forgiving and retaining sins: *i.e.* of exercising that equity in discipline which so exasperated the rigorist Tertullian.[2] Episcopal not papal authority was, as yet, the question at stake: and for the first application of the Petrine text to the papal claims, so far as our evidence goes, we must pass on to the period of Cyprian, bishop of Carthage, 248-†58, and Pope Stephen, 254-†7. By this time, St. Paul had disappeared; except in so far as his memory was venerated by our English forefathers when they made their pilgrimages *ad limina beatorum apostolorum* in Rome.[3]

---

[1] Eus., *H. E.* V. xxviii. 3.
[2] Tert., *De pudicitia*, c. xxi: Mirbt[4], No. 55.
[3] Bede, *Eccl. Hist.*: v. c. 7.

CHAPTER III

CYPRIAN AND STEPHEN

§ 1. CYPRIAN became bishop of Carthage in 248; and during the persecution of Decius, January-November 250, he had to deal with some of the lapsed, who informed him that they desired to be reconciled to the Church without delay and that, for that purpose, they themselves were the Church. He proceeded to read them a lesson about the constitution of the Church. " Our Lord," he writes,[1] " determining the office of a bishop and the ordering of His own Church, speaks in the Gospel and says to Peter: ' I say unto thee that thou art Peter and upon this rock I will build my Church, and the gates of hell shall not prevail against it: and I will give unto thee the keys of the kingdom of heaven, and whatsoever thou shalt bind upon earth shall be bound in heaven, and whatsoever thou shalt loose upon earth shall be loosed in heaven.' Thence the ordination of bishops and the ordering of the Church runs down along the course of time and line of succession, so that the Church is settled upon her bishops; and every act of the Church is regulated by these same prelates." This was sufficient answer to such of its members as claimed to act " in the name of the Church," *i.e.* the local church of Carthage: whereas " a church

---

[1] Cyprian, *Ep.* xxxiii. § 1: Mirbt[4], No. 68.

consists of the bishop and clergy and all who stand,"
i.e. the faithful laity.

§ 2. The letter is noteworthy, in the present connexion, because Cyprian here takes the *Tu es Petrus* as
the charter not of the papacy but of the episcopate.
Shortly afterwards, five presbyters, who had resented
his election as bishop of Carthage, supported by a
wealthy layman named Felicissimus, made a bid for
the interest of the lapsed by promising them immediate
reconciliation. An anti-Cyprianic party thus arose,
which presently developed into a schism: and, since
excommunication had no terrors for men who had
already withdrawn from communion of their own
accord, Cyprian could only deal with the situation by
expounding again the constitution of the Church. Not
long before Easter,[1] 23rd March, 251, he wrote to his
people to warn them against " the faction of Felicissimus "[2] and explained that in each Christian community
there can be but one church, one episcopal chair, and
one altar. " They now offer peace, who themselves
have not peace. They now promise to bring back and
restore the lapsed to the church who have themselves
departed from the church. There is one God, and
one Christ, and one church and one chair founded by
the Word of the Lord on Peter."[3] How the foundation
of the Church upon Peter has for its consequence the
unity of government and worship in each community, or
how such unity depends upon Peter, Cyprian does not
in his letter to his people think it necessary to explain.

[1] *Ep.* xliii. § 7.   [2] *Ib.* § 2.
[3] *Ib.* § 5.

But in his treatise on *The Unity of the Church*,[1] written about the same time and read within a month,[2] to a Council of Bishops at Carthage, on 1st April, 251, he sets out his theory in full.[3] " § 4. The Lord saith unto Peter: ' I say unto thee that thou art Peter,' etc. . . . Upon him, being one, He builds His Church; and, though He gives to all the Apostles an equal power, and says ' As my Father sent me, even so send I you; receive ye the Holy Ghost; whosesoever sins ye remit, they shall be remitted to him, and whosesoever sins ye retain, they shall be retained '; yet, in order to manifest unity, He has by His own authority, so placed the source of the same unity as to begin from one. Certainly, the other apostles also were what Peter was, endued with an equal fellowship of office[4] and power; but a commencement is made from unity, that the Church may be set before us as one . . . He who holds not this unity of the Church, does he think that he holds the faith ? He who strives against and resists the Church, is he assured that he is in the Church . . . § 5. This unity we should firmly hold and maintain: especially we bishops, in order that we may approve the episcopate itself to be one and undivided . . . The episcopate is one; it is a whole in which each enjoys full

[1] *De catholicæ ecclesiæ unitate* (*Op.* iii. 209-33: ed. Hartel): Mirbt[4], No. 66.

[2] *Ep.* liv. § 4 and *Doc. Ch. Hist.* i., No. 147.

[3] For the interpolations, see *Opera* (ed. Hartel) i. 212, and Mirbt[4], No. 66. They are first found in a letter of Pope Pelagius II to the bishops of Istria, c. 585 (see Jaffé, *Regesta*[2] 1055), and on them see E. Denny, *Papalism*, § 1239, and P. Batiffol, *L'Église naissante*, Excursus E.

[4] ' honoris ': so translated by W. Bright. *The Roman See in the Early Church*, 43: and *cf.* the Cursus honorum.

possession."[1]   At times, Cyprian treats the unity of
the episcopate as resulting from a common mind
amongst its members.[2]   But it goes deeper than this;
and is inherent in the conception of the episcopate as
a tenure upon a totality in which each bishop possesses
that full authority which, according to Cyprian, our
Lord first conferred upon Peter.   For a time, Peter was
its sole depositary.   Then the same powers, to bind
and to loose, were conferred upon his colleagues.   But
he enjoyed them first, so as to become once and for
all not a centre but a symbol of unity: with the result
that the *Tu es Petrus* is the charter of episcopal authority
and the *Cathedra Petri* a compendious description of
the authority which each and every bishop enjoys.
Thus there is but " one chair founded on Peter by the
word of the Lord ":[3] and every bishop is Peter's successor, enthroned as such in Peter's chair.   Such is
the African theory.   " It is not clear here whether the
' one chair ' is the Roman see or the episcopate as a
whole; the context suggests the latter.   But, if so, the
one episcopate, like the one Church, is to Cyprian in
intimate relation of dependence on the one person of
St. Peter:"[4] to the exclusion of St. Paul.   By the
exclusive prominence thus given to St. Peter, the
language of St. Cyprian aided in the development of

[1] Episcopatus unus est, cujus a singulis in solidum pars
tenetur, § 5.

[2] *E.g.*, Ecclesia, quæ catholica una est, scissa non sit
neque divisa, sed sit utique connexa et cohærentium sibi
invicem glutino copulata.   *Ep.* lxvi. § 8: Mirbt[4], No. 72:
and *cf. Ep.* liv. § 24; lxviii. § 3.

[3] *Ep.* xliii. § 5.

[4] C. H. Turner, *Catholic and Apostolic*, 228.

the papalist theory: and the *Tu es Petrus* of Mt. xvi. 18, 19 as well as the other two Petrine texts (Lk. xxii. 31 : John xxi. 16) are certainly patient of the Roman interpretation. But the place occupied in Christian thought and history by the African theory, assigning as it does no less authority to the episcopate than to Peter, is enough to shew that these words of our Lord do not necessitate it.

The theory persists with Optatus, bishop of Mileve in Numidia, *c.* 370. In a well-known passage of his *De schismate Donatistarum*[1] " he is arguing against the Donatists who had schismatically intruded bishops of their own into sees already canonically occupied, amongst which was that of Rome. As an African, he held the view " of St. Cyprian " that St. Peter was the representative of the whole episcopate. Hence the ' See of Peter ' (Langen) ' is the one ecclesiastical see in which all the apostles and their successors the bishops in equal measure participate, which is called after Peter because he first (to emphasize symbolically the unity of the Church) was put in possession of it ': thus ' the Sees of all the churches are, equally, different representatives of the one whole See.' "[2] But among the sees into which the Donatists had intruded bishops of their own was the see of Rome itself: and Optatus gives the names of the intruding succession.[3] He takes this intrusion into St. Peter's own chair—the actual chair in which he was (by that date) supposed to have

---

[1] Optatus, *De schismate Donatistarum* ii. cc. 2, 3 (C.S.E.L. xxvi): Mirbt[4], No. 130.
[2] Denny, *Papalism*, § 865.   [3] Optatus, ii. c. 4.

sat—as the simplest example of their daring: and his argument is that " inasmuch as the episcopal commission was first bestowed upon Peter in order that the unity of the Church might be symbolised, and so divisions amongst the apostles and their successors prevented, therefore to set up a chair against that one chair would be evil; consequently the act of the Donatists in doing so at Rome proclaimed them to be schismatics; his argument being emphasised and rendered more pointed by the fact that the Apostle who represented in his person the One Episcopate had already sat in the episcopal chair of that city. His argument refers solely to the position of the Catholic episcopate as against that of the Donatists, and has no reference whatever to any unique sovereign position belonging to the bishop of Rome."[1] Or, to put it shortly, " Optatus was arguing merely about the state of the Church in the city of Rome, and said that the Petrine succession was the Catholic one in Rome, and that the Donatist bishops there are schismatic: not a word about the Papacy."[2]

§ 3. Cyprian also quite naturally acknowledges that there is a sense in which the title *Cathedra Petri* belongs more specifically to the Roman See (supposing of course, though facts, as we have seen, are against it, that St. Peter was ever bishop of Rome) as well as a sense in which the African Church owes its *unitas sacerdotalis*, or episcopate, to Rome as to the " princi-

---

[1] Denny, §§ 866-7.
[2] Church Historical Society: Tract No. xiv. On the *Satis cognitum* of Leo XIII: p. 18.

pal " or mother-church.[1] But nevertheless, it is with Carthage and not with Rome that the local schismatics must finally deal " since it has been decreed by our whole body, and is alike equitable and just, that every cause should be heard there where the offence has been committed." So Cyprian in the spring of A.D. 252. Two years later Stephen became bishop of Rome: and relations between Rome and Africa bear further upon the conception of the Roman primacy then current.

§ 4. In Spain, two bishops had apostatized in the persecution. They were Basilides and Martialis; and their two sees Merida and Leon-with-Astorga: though it is not certain which is to be assigned to each. Basilides, " in some sickness, blasphemed God "[2] and resigned. He was succeeded in the see by Sabinus, duly elected by the people and consecrated by the neighbouring bishops.[3] Martialis, besides his lapse, joined a pagan guild (collegium), took part in its banquets, and buried his sons in its grounds.[4] The two prelates then went off to Rome, and implored Stephen to restore them to their respective sees. The Pope allowed himself to be imposed upon, and re-instated them. Thereupon Felix, a presbyter, with the laity of Leon-

---

[1] After acknowledging Pope Cornelius 251-†3 as the legitimate bishop of Rome (Ep. lix. § 5) Cyprian goes on to say of the Donatists that, after setting up for themselves a pseudo-bishop ordained for them by heretics, " navigare audent et ad Petri cathedram atque ad ecclesiam principalem, unde unitas sacerdotalis exorta est, ab schismaticis et profanis litteras ferre nec cogitare eos esse Romanos quorum fides apostolo praedicante (Rom i. 8) laudata est ad quos perfidia habere non possit accessum " (§ 14): Mirbt⁴, No. 70. Note, too, " exorta est," not " exoritur."

[2] Ep. lxvii. § 6.   [3] Ib. § 5.   [4] Ib. § 6.

and-Astorga, and Aelius, a deacon, with the people of
Merida, as well as Sabinus and another Felix [possibly
bishop] of Saragossa, brought the case to the notice
of Cyprian. A synod of bishops, 254, addressed an
epistle to the Spanish churches, affirming the validity
of the consecration of Sabinus and Felix.[1] They
ignore the papal decision, but exculpate Stephen on
the ground of ignorance. It does not look as if either
the church of Spain or the church of Africa took the
Roman see as more than one among other influential
sees; or held recourse to Rome to be of any more consequence than recourse to Carthage.

§ 5. Rather late in 254, Cyprian addressed a letter[2]
to Pope Stephen about the case of Marcian, Bishop of
Arles in Gaul. There was, as yet, no metropolitan
in Gaul: but Arles and Lyons, being in the same
Provincia Narbonensis, Faustinus, Bishop of Lyons,
in his own name and in the name of his colleagues,
wrote both to Stephen and to Cyprian to inform them
of Marcian's lapse into schism by joining the Novatianists.[3] They were the two metropolitans of the
West. Stephen appears to have taken no action.
Whereupon Cyprian, having received a second request
from Faustinus, wrote rather peremptorily to Stephen,
reminding him of the duty of the episcopate to intervene
in such a case, and urging him on its behalf to " write
fully to the bishops of the Province and the laity of
Arles so that after Marcian has been excommunicated
another [bishop] may be substituted in his place."[4]

[1] *Ep*. lxvii. §5.   [2] *Ep*. lxviii.
[3] *Ib*. § 1.   [4] *Ib*. § 3.

Then let Stephen " signify plainly to us who has been substituted in the place of Marcian."[1] It might look as if Cyprian expected Stephen to act as Pope, and to deal with Marcian by his own supreme authority. It is true that he appeals to " the weight and authority " of his see. But this he owes to his martyr-predecessors, Cornelius and Lucius.[2] It is also true that Stephen is called upon to act as first of the bishops of Christendom, and in their name; though this is not said explicitly. The simple reasons for Stephen's intervention are such as that Rome lay nearer to Gaul than did Carthage; that several of the Gallic sees owed their origin to Rome, and some quite recently, and that, if the honour of the episcopate were to be vindicated against Marcian, which is what Cyprian demands, it was for the bishop of Rome, as first among bishops, to act on its behalf. On the other hand, it was for the local bishops of the Province, thus supported, both to excommunicate Marcian and, with the laity, to appoint his successor. Then Stephen would come in again to send round the name of the bishop.

§ 6. Shortly afterwards, in the controversy about heretical baptism between Cyprian and Stephen, we come across the first known instance of a Pope appealing to the Petrine text as the basis of his supreme authority —" Stephen, who boasts of the seat of his episcopate and contends that he holds the succession from Peter, on whom the foundations of the Church were laid."[3]

About 213, Agrippinus, bishop of Carthage, at a

[1] *Ep*. lxviii. § 5.　　　　　　[2] *Ib*. § 5.
[3] *Ep*. lxxv. § 17.

Council of some seventy bishops of Proconsular Africa
and Numidia, ruled that those who had been baptized
by schismatics must be baptized anew before they could
be reconciled to the Catholic Church.[1]   In the Roman
church, on the contrary, the tradition was clear and
continuous against rebaptism: they were admitted
simply by the laying on of hands.   Early in 255 some
bishops of Numidia, relying upon the Roman usage,[2]
dispensed with baptism in the case of converts from
heresy or schism.[3]   Eighteen of their colleagues dis-
agreed, and reported the matter to Cyprian.   He
referred the question to his synod.   It was the *First
Council of Carthage on Baptism*, and met in the spring
of 255, with thirty-two bishops of Proconsular Africa
in attendance.   In their name, Cyprian wrote a reply
to the Numidians.[4]   Relying upon the African form
of the baptismal creed— " Dost thou believe in eternal
life, and remission of sins through the holy Church ?"[5]
—he takes the view that, as remission of sins is not
given except in the Church, heretics must needs be
baptized in order to be admitted to it.[6]   They must
also be confirmed; for " there is but one baptism, and
one [bestowal of the] Holy Spirit and one Church
founded by Christ our Lord upon Peter."[7]   The
Numidians may have been convinced by Cyprian's
reply; and Cyprian may have thought that opposition
to the Carthaginian custom was confined to a corner

---

[1] *Ep*. lxxi. § 4: Mirbt[4], No. 76.   [2] *Ep*. lxxv. § 6.
[3] *Ep*. lxx. § 1.   [4] *Ep*. lxx.: Mirbt[4], No. 77A.
[5] Hahn, *Symbole*[3], § 12.
[6] *Ep*. lxx. § 2: *Doc. Ch. Hist*. i., No. 153.
[7] *Ib*. § 3.

of Africa. But, if so, Quintus, a bishop of Mauretania,[1] undeceived him. Rome, he wrote, was opposed to the repetition of baptism. This was startling news; and Cyprian replied[2] by sending him the letter[3] of his *First Council on Baptism*.[4] Let Rome, he says, give up its appeal to " custom " and listen to " reason," as Peter did to Paul at Antioch, " making no such insolent claim for himself as to say that he held the primacy, and should rather be obeyed of those late and newly come."[5] He then prepared to deal with Rome itself; and, before Easter 256, at the *Second Council of Carthage on Baptism*, attended by seventy-one bishops of Proconsular Africa and Numidia, he addressed a letter in their name to Stephen.[6] Here he re-affirms the African position that those baptized in heresy or schism must be rebaptized; for such baptism is no baptism as will appear from the letters[7] enclosed.[8] Meanwhile differences of custom are no bar to communion. We do not lay down any law, since each bishop is master in his own house.[9] We do not possess Stephen's reply in its entirety: but, as quoted by Cyprian in a letter to Pompey, bishop of Sabrata in Tripoli,[10] the Pope, in answer to the invitation to modify the Roman usage, held that we ought not to be more exacting than the heretics (for they do not rebaptize converts who go over to them) and lays down the law—" If then any

<hr />

[1] *Ep.* lxxii. § 1.
[2] *Ep.* lxxi.
[3] *Ep.* lxx.
[4] *Ep.* lxxi. § 1.
[5] *Ib.* § 3: Mirbt⁴, No. 76.
[6] *Ep.* lxxii.
[7] *Epp.* lxx., lxxi.
[8] *Ep.* lxxii. § 1.
[9] *Ib.* § 3.
[10] *Ep.* lxxiv.: Mirbt⁴, No. 78: *Doc. Ch. Hist.* i., No. 149.

shall come to you from any heresy whatsoever, let there
be no innovations beyond what has been handed
down."[1] As to Cyprian's request that Stephen
should keep his custom, let each bishop be answerable
to God only, and meanwhile live in peace and concord
with his brethren who thought otherwise, Stephen
met it with a threat of excommunication.[2]

In Mauretania, however, there were bishops who
held with Stephen,[3] that not even such as come over
from Marcion were to be rebaptized. Their opinion
was brought to the notice of Cyprian by one of their
number, Jubaianus; and Cyprian sent him a long
explanation,[4] which is " the most important document
on the theory of the question."[5] So indeed it appears
to have been regarded by Jubaianus, for he gave his
assent; and so too by the bishops who assembled,
1st Sept., 256, for the *Third Council of Carthage on
Baptism*. They were eighty-seven in number from Proconsular Africa, Numidia and Mauretania. Cyprian,
in his introductory address, referred to the correspondence with Jubaianus; and then proceeded:—
" It remains that we severally declare our opinion,
judging no one, nor depriving any one of the right of
communion if he differs from us. For no one of us
setteth himself up as a bishop of bishops, or by a
tyrannical terror forceth his colleagues to a necessity

---

[1] Nihil innovetur nisi quod traditum est: *Ep*. lxxiv. § 1.
[2] Abstinendos (*sc*. bishops who took Cyprian's line)
putat: *ib*. § 8.
[3] *Epp*. lxxii. § 7, lxxiii. § 4.
[4] *Ep*. lxxiii.: Mirbt[4], No. 77 B: *Doc. Ch. Hist*. i., No. 156.
[5] L. Duchesne, *Early History of the Church*, i. 308.

of obeying."[1]   Stephen was not mentioned, but every
one understood, and they gave their " opinions " in
support of their Primate.   They then sent a deputation,
Sept., 256, to Rome with a letter from Cyprian, who
waited on Stephen, but were not received.[2]   On the
contrary, the Pope replied,[3] not merely claiming authority for the Roman usage,[4] but magnifying his office as
that of the successor of Peter and occupant of Peter's
Chair.[5]   It is the first occasion on record on which the
claim was made.   " Pope Stephen then affirmed the
primacy of the see of Rome, a primacy going back
to St. Peter, and a primacy giving to the bishop
of Rome an authority over the other bishops of
Christendom."[6]

§ 7. Meanwhile, Cyprian had informed the bishops
of the chief sees about the course of the controversy
with Stephen; and reactions took place in the East.
There the traditions of Alexandria and Palestine were
the same as that of Rome: whereas synodical decisions
in Asia and Syria had ranged these regions on the same
side as Cyprian.[7]   One of many replies to Cyprian's
information was that of Firmilian, bishop of Cæsarea
in Cappadocia, 232-†72, in a letter translated by
Cyprian himself and preserved in his correspondence.[8]
Its tone is injurious; as that of Cyprian and Stephen to
each other had already become.   But, allowing for

---

[1] *Sententiæ Episcoporum*: *Cypriani Op.* i. 435 sq. (ed.
Hartel): Mirbt[4], No. 79.
[2] *Ep.* lxxv. § 25.   [3] *Ep.* lxxiv. § 1.
[4] *Ep.* lxxv. §§ 5, 6.   [5] *Ib.* § 17: Mirbt[4], No. 81.
[6] Batiffol, *L'Église naissante*[5], 469.
[7] *Ep.* lxxv. § 19.   [8] *Ep.* lxxv.

such regrettable developments, Firmilian's contribution
is notable. As for the stress laid by Stephen, he says,
upon the maintenance of tradition, Stephen's predecessors (from the point of view of Asia) were none too
careful of it, as in the paschal controversy.[1] In spite
of differences, however, between Rome and Asia,
there was not then any breach of communion; nor has
there been since, till Stephen " broke the peace "
with Africa,[2] parading his Petrine authority[3] with the
result that, in thinking to excommunicate others, he
has only succeeded in excommunicating himself![4]
Wild words to a Pope; and inconceivable if the Roman
primacy had then been thought to carry with it universal jurisdiction.

But the storm was allayed by the milder counsel of
Dionysius, bishop of Alexandria 247-†65; who played
the part with Stephen which Irenæus had so happily
assumed with Victor. He took the line that " heretics
may be validly admitted without baptism, but that
churches which ruled otherwise must not be overruled
from without."[5] The controversy gradually died away;
but its interest in reference to the Roman primacy is
that it brought the earliest stages in the use of the
Tu es Petrus to a term: " Callistus, in his celebrated
' peremptory edict,'[6] had made use of the text, *Tu es
Petrus ;* but, as far as the citation by Tertullian allows

---

[1] *Ep.* lxxv. §§ 5, 6.　　　　　　[2] *Ib.* § 6.
[3] *Ib.* § 17.
[4] *Ib.* § 24: *Doc. Ch. Hist.* i., No. 155.
[5] Eus., *H.E.* VII. vii. §§ 4, 5: as summarized in E. W.
Benson, *Cyprian* 137.
[6] Tert.. *De pudicitia*, c. 14: Mirbt[4], No. 54.

us to judge of it, he only claimed the episcopal right to remit sins. St. Cyprian, rather later, made use of it to prove the divine origin and the rights of the episcopate. Stephen was the first, as we know from Firmilian, to employ the *Tu es Petrus* in the service of the primacy."[1]

[1] J. Turmel, *Dogme de la papauté*, 176.

CHAPTER IV

ALEXANDRIA AND ANTIOCH

IN the latter half of the third century events are few. But the centralization of the Church round the great sees of Rome, Alexandria and Antioch made silent growth; and two incidents, each connected with the name of Dionysius, bishop of Alexandria,[1] †275, bear witness to it.

§ 1. In the Libyan Pentapolis, which lay within his jurisdiction,[2] Sabellianism had made much progress. Already, in 257, he had called the attention of Pope Sixtus II to it.[3] Presently, he felt bound to intervene; and, in a letter of 260, he set himself to explain. His opponents laid complaint against him before his namesake, Dionysius, bishop of Rome, 259-†68; not without reason, as it would seem. For, in the endeavour to counter Sabellianism by emphasizing the distinctness of the Son from the Father, he had overstated the Filial Subordination.[4] The Roman bishop consulted his synod; and then wrote two letters. One ran in the name of the synod and was addressed to the Church of Alexandria;[5] correcting his views but without mention

---

[1] See *The Letters of Dionysius of Alexandria*: ed. C. L. Feltoe (Cambridge University Press, 1904), pp. 165 sqq.
[2] Athanasius, *De sententia Dionysii*, § 5.
[3] Eus., *H.E.* VII. vi.
[4] Ath., *De sent. Dio.* § 4.
[5] Ath., *De decretis* § 26: Feltoe, 177 sqq.

of his name. The other was a private letter to Dionysius himself, asking for an explanation. It was readily given in his *Elenchus et apologia*.[1] We are not now concerned with the theological question at issue, but only with the incident in its bearing upon the Roman primacy.

The facts are, briefly, three. When the opponents of Dionysius of Alexandria wanted aid against him, they had recourse not to a synod of local bishops but to the Roman see. The Roman bishop took up the case and asked for an explanation. The explanation was promptly given. The question is, therefore, whether the letter of Dionysius of Rome was simply the request of one co-trustee to another for an explanation of his colleagues' action in a matter concerning their common trust ? Or, whether it was coupled with an assumption of jurisdiction parallel to that in the letter of the bishop of Alexandria to the bishops of Libya ? The answer turns upon considerations such as the following. First, the fragment of the letter of Dionysius of Rome tells us nothing of the form of intervention, nor is there any positive evidence in either document for any assumption of jurisdiction. Secondly, Dionysius of Alexandria replied, indeed, to the written inquiries of his namesake; but the fragments of his answer shew that he wrote from a position of independence, nor is there anything of the narrative of Athanasius which implies that the Alexandrian bishop recognized, or that the Roman bishop claimed, authoritative jurisdiction in this case as belonging to the

[1] Feltoe, 182 sqq.

Roman See. Thirdly, in dealing with previous
" popes " of Rome, the " pope " of Alexandria had
" entreated "[1] Stephen, and had asked Sixtus for his
" opinion."[2]   But his " entreaties " were characteristic
of his good manners and conciliatory temper; and it was
the " advice " of a " brother " that he wanted to have.

Nevertheless, the recourse of the Alexandrians to
the Roman bishop was not lost upon his successors,
nor upon those who sought his aid.   Julius I, 337-†52,
in his letter to the Eusebians at Antioch, 340, had it
clearly in mind when claiming a peculiar prerogative
for his see over the affairs of " the church of the
Alexandrians ";[3] and it was equally in the mind of
their patriarch Cyril when, in the case of Nestorius,
he also wrote, about April, 430, of there being a " custom " in favour of reference to the Roman see.[4]   It
was too good a precedent for Rome, and those who
sought her assistance, not to turn it to account.[5]

§ 2. The second incident of this epoch, bearing
upon the Roman primacy, is the case of Paul of Samosata, bishop of Antioch, c. 260-72.   He was an adoptian-
ist in doctrine, and held that our Lord was a mere
man—" from below "; not " from above," as St. John
says.[6]   Three synods of neighbouring bishops were
held, 264-9, to deal with him; and to the first of these
Dionysius of Alexandria was invited, but unable
through old age to attend.   He gave his views in
writing,[7] and, thus supported, the synod of 269 at

---

[1] Eus., *H.E.* VII. v. § 5.   [2] *Ib.* VII. ix. § 2.
[3] Ath., *Apol. c. Ar.* § 35.   [4] *Ep.* xi. § 1.
[5] Kidd, *Hist. Ch. to A.D.* 461, i. 489 sq.
[6] St. John iii. 31.   [7] Eus., *H.E.* VII. xxvii. § 2

last deposed Paul. But they could not turn him out of the house belonging to the see, till after the fall of his patroness Zenobia and an appeal to the Emperor Aurelian. The Emperor ordered " the house to be given up to those to whom the bishops of Italy and of the city of the Romans should assign it."[1] His test, it will be observed, is that of recognition by the bishops " of the religion " in Italy and Rome: not communion with the bishop of Rome only, for papalism was unknown in Aurelian's day.

Rome, however, was supreme in Italy, as Alexandria in Egypt, while Antioch had its rights in its own region called The East. It was this state of things that was recognized by the sixth canon[2] of the Council of Nicæa, 325—" Let the ancient customs prevail." According to this canon, the most important of the series, " the authority which the Council contemplated as customarily belonging to the Roman bishop is analogous to that which was to be retained by the Alexandrian . . . If the Nicene fathers had recognized what is called the ' papal supremacy,' they could not but have noticed it in this canon. For they were considering the subject of authority, and of such authority as was held, in different areas, by Rome and Alexandria alike . . . The omission is a proof, if proof were wanted, that the First Œcumenical Council knew nothing of the doctrine of papal supremacy."[3]

[1] *Ib.* VII. xxx. § 19: Mirbt[4], No. 85: *Doc. Ch. Hist.* i., No. 184.
[2] Mirbt[4], No. 111: *Doc. Ch. Hist.* ii., No. 11.
[3] W. Bright, *Notes on the Canons*: Nic. 6.

CHAPTER V

CONSTANTINE AND HIS SONS

ROME, however, had its primacy everywhere admitted; and our next task is to see how far, during the dominance of Constantine †337 and Constantius †361, a modification was introduced into this state of things. The part taken, or the treatment suffered, by the papacy during the struggle first with Donatism and then with Arianism will serve to shew what measure of its prestige survived.

§ 1. Donatism was a schism which originated in Africa on the appointment of Cæcilian, 311, to be bishop of Carthage. A party of malcontents was formed against him. They held his consecration to be invalid, alleging that Felix, bishop of Aptunga, one of his consecrators, had given up the Scriptures in the late persecution and so was a *Traditor.* It was a charge that involved two questions. First, a question of fact: Was Felix a *Traditor*, or was he not ? Second, a question of doctrine: If he was, does the unworthiness of the minister hinder the effect of the sacrament ? We are not here concerned with the merits of the controversy; only with its bearing on the Roman primacy during the reign of Constantine. On 15th April, 313 a complaint was made against Cæcilian *a parte Majorini* (the Donatist leader previous to that Donatus

from whom the party took its name) in a letter[1] addressed
to the Emperor. They besought him to appoint judges
from Gaul to consider their grievance; for in Gaul
there had been no persecution, and, therefore, the crime
of giving up the Scriptures had been there unknown.
Constantine, master of the West, who was quick to
scent danger to peace and unity, took up the petition
and referred it to a Council at Rome,[2] 2-4 Oct., 313,
where Miltiades, bishop of Rome, with three Gallic
bishops was required to look into the question. They
gave their decision in favour of Cæcilian. But his
opponents made fresh complaint, on the ground that
the Roman synod had never gone into the question
which lay at the root of the matter, viz. the alleged
offence of Felix, the consecrator of Cæcilian. Constantine therefore ordered further inquiry to be held,
on this point. A second,[3] and then a third, investigation followed, the latter at the Council of Arles,
1st Aug., 314. It was a synod completely representative
of the West. Cæcilian was once more cleared, and the
Council reported[4] its proceedings to Pope Sylvester,
314-†37. They paid him great deference: " We
salute thee with the reverence that is thy due, most
glorious Pope," and then continued, " We agreed to
write to you who hold the greater dioceses that by
you especially our decrees should be brought to the

[1] Optatus, *De schismate Donatistarum* i. § 22 (*C.S.E.L.*
xxvi. 25) and *Doc. Ch. Hist.* i., No. 197.

[2] Constantine to Miltiades: Eus., *H.E.* X. v. §§ 18-20:
Doc. Ch. Hist. i., No. 191: Mirbt[4], No. 96.

[3] On 15th Feb., 314, at Carthage: *Doc. Ch. Hist.*, No. 199.

[4] *Ib.* No. 201: Mirbt[4], No. 100.

knowledge of all." The term " Diocese " is here used apparently in the civil sense of the subdivision of a Præfecture, and " the greater dioceses " are then those of the later Præfecture of Italy, including Africa and Illyricum, which covered a larger area than those of the regions where the Council met, viz. the dioceses of Gaul, Spain and Britain, afterwards making up the Præfecture of Gaul. The former were apparently regarded at this date as under the especial care of the Pope, but his primacy is clearly acknowledged as accepted throughout the West. But in what sense ? The Pope is not asked for a decision, nor to confirm the proceedings of the Council, for the Council itself had given its decision: " We thought well, in the presence of the Holy Spirit and His Angels, that we should make some decrees to provide for the present state of tranquillity." Sylvester is merely asked to make these decrees known, precisely as Cyprian had asked Stephen to send round word as to who had been elected bishop in the place of Marcian, bishop of Arles. Thus, a chief function of the primacy was still, at this date, to be the centre of communications—not of communion—between the several churches of the West, as later to represent the churches of the West in communications with the churches of the East. It was still a primacy, but far, as yet, from a supremacy, and the final sentence against Donatism was given not by the Pope, but by the Emperor himself in a fourth investigation held at Milan,[1] 10th Nov., 316.

[1] Aug., *Contra Cresconium* iii. § 82: *Doc. Ch. Hist.* i., No. 219.

§ 2. Arianism, like Donatism, was a disturbance that threatened the peace and unity of the Empire: and for this reason attracted the attention of Constantine. At the suggestion of his ecclesiastical adviser[1] Hosius, bishop of Cordova 296-†357, the Emperor, in a letter of invitation to the bishops,[2] designated Nicæa as the place of assembly for a General Council, which was held there, May-June, 325. It was the Emperor too who imposed the decisive formula " Of one substance with the Father,"[3] and it was he who had summoned the Council, as we learn from his letter to the Church of Alexandria[4] and as the Council itself records in its letter to that Church.[5]

At a banquet at which Constantine entertained a company of bishops,[6] possibly those of the Council, to celebrate his *Vicennalia*,[7] 25th July, 325, he let fall the remark—in the half-serious tone of an after-dinner speaker—" You, my Lords, are bishops in charge of the internal affairs of the Church, I am appointed by God to be bishop of her relations with the world at large." But, in dealing with the affair whether of Donatism or of Nicæa, the bishop of her external relations was transformed into the bishop of her internal affairs. They were to him affairs of State. As compared with the Emperor, the Pope counted for nothing. For at Arles Constantine revised a decision given by

---

[1] Rufinus, *H. E.* i. c. 1; Sulpitius Severus, *Hist. Sacr.* i. c. 40.
[2] Hefele, *Conciles* i. 403.
[3] Theodoret, *H.E.* I. xii. § 7.
[4] Socrates, *H.E.* I. ix. § 19.   [5] *Ib.* § 2.
[6] Eus., *V.C.* iv. c. 24.   [7] *Ib.* iv. c. 15.

Pope Miltiades, and his Council at Rome, and then revised both Rome and Arles again by his own definitive sentence at Milan; while he so dominated the proceedings at Nicæa that, early in the sixth century, a new account was invented, and repeated at the Sixth General Council,[1] 680, that Constantine had summoned the Council in concert with Pope Sylvester. Similarly, it was alleged by a Council of Rome, 5th Oct., 485, that the proceedings of Nicæa were confirmed by the authority of the Roman church.[2] These later statements, however, are of little worth, and so is the story of Sylvester having presided by his deputies. For Hosius was president, whether by choice of the Emperor or in virtue of his personal pre-eminence. He signed first, and the papal legates, Vito and Vincentius, appended their signatures next. In short, during all these years, Constantine ignored the papacy, and then left a legacy most injurious to its prestige by raising up three influences adverse to it. They were (1) the Court Bishops, (2) the Prince-Theologians and (3) the see of Constantinople, which, after forty years of Arianism, aspired to become New Rome in more than name.

§ 3. We come now to the Council of Sardica, 343, which marks an epoch, as in the repudiation of Arianism, so in the recovery of the prestige of the Roman see.

On the death of Constantine, 22nd May, 337, his empire was partitioned between his three sons, Constantine II †340, and Constans †350, in the West and

---

[1] Labbé-Cossart, *Concilia* vii. 1086 B.
[2] Hefele, *Councils* i. 44.

Constantius II †361, in the East, who by the death of Constans became sole Emperor, 351-61. In the later years of Constantine there had been an Arianising reaction led by the Court bishops at the head of whom stood Eusebius, bishop, at first, of Nicomedia 325-39, and then of Constantinople, 339-†42. At the Council of Tyre, 335, they succeeded in deposing Athanasius and procuring his exile to Trèves, 336-7, but Constantine II, on the death of his father, sent him back to Alexandria, where he resumed his see. Toward the end of 338 the Eusebians, in the hope of enlisting the support of the Roman see, sent an embassy to Pope Julius I, 337-†52, with a number of charges against Athanasius and a request for a Council.[1] Julius sent the *dossier* to Athenasius,[2] who, finding himself in danger at Alexandria, took refuge in Rome, where he arrived March, 339. The Pope then sent envoys to invite the Eusebians to Rome.[3] But they detained his representatives, and, at a Council of Antioch, Jan., 340, prepared a reply in terms of " polished irony," as Sozomen says, to the effect that " the church of Rome was a home of Apostles and had become the metropolis of religion from the first, although those who had introduced it there had come from the East. And they took it amiss that the second place of honour should be assigned to them just because they had not the advantage of size or numbers in their church, whereas they excelled the Romans in virtue and loyalty."[4] So

---

[1] Ath., *Apol. c. Ar.* § 22. [2] *Ib.* § 83.
[3] Ath., *Hist. Ar.* § 11.
[4] Sozomen, *H.E.* III. viii. §§ 44-8.

saying, they sent back the envoys of Pope Julius, and declined to attend his Council, on the further plea that they were prevented by the Persian War from so doing.[1]

Julius now felt that the time had come for him to take action, and, at a Council of Rome, Oct.-Nov., 340, Athanasius was declared innocent[2] and Marcellus of Ancyra orthodox[3] on his acceptance of the old Roman Creed.[4] These decisions, at the request of the Council, were then notified by Pope Julius in a letter[5] rightly regarded as one of the ablest and most important documents which have ever emanated from the Roman see. The Pope says that he writes not in his own name but in the name of his colleagues as well.[6] " Supposing that some offence rested upon these persons—Athanasius and Marcellus—the case ought to have been conducted against them not after this manner but according to the canon of the Church. Word should have been written of it to us all, so that a just sentence might have proceeded from all," *i.e.* from the episcopate acting as a body, so far is Julius from claiming the prerogative of judging by himself alone. " For," he continues, " the sufferers were bishops and churches of no ordinary note but those which the Apostles themselves had governed in their own persons "—St. Peter, so it was held, through his disciple St. Mark, at Alex-

---

[1] Ath., *Apol. c. Ar.* § 25.   [2] *Ib.* § 20.
[3] *Apol. c. Ar.* § 32.
[4] *Doc. Ch. Hist.* i., No. 204.
[5] Ath., *Apol. c. Ar.* §§ 21-35: Mirbt[4], No. 121: *Doc. Ch. Hist.* ii., No. 17.
[6] *Apol. c. Ar.* § 25.

andria and St. Paul at Ancyra. Then follows a further
point, about the claim of Rome to a peculiar authority
in the case of Alexandria. "And why was nothing
said to us concerning the church of the Alexandrians
in particular ? Are you not aware that the custom has
been for word to be written first to us; and so, after
that,[1] for a just decision to be passed ?"[2] The
canon supposed to govern the case of bishops of Apostolic Sees was entirely misrepresented by Socrates[3]
and Sozomen[4] as well as by St. Leo.[5] Thence the
mistake found its way into the *Decreta* of Pope
Julius *cc.* v., vi., included in the *Forged Decretals*,[6] of
the ninth century, and so became one of the supports
traditionally alleged in favour of the papal claim to be
the sole and final judge. But what Julius actually
claimed was: (*a*) that, in the case of bishops of Apostolic
Sees, the canon requires that questions relating to
them should be referred to the episcopate as a whole;
and (*b*) that, in a case concerning the bishop of Alexandria, custom requires that such authority should be
reserved to the Roman see as Dionysius of Rome
exercised in dealing with complaints against Dionysius
of Alexandria. Julius, in fact, was much too modest
about his primacy for his words to be quoted in evi-

---

[1] καὶ οὕτως ἔνθεν = *et sic deinde* (see Dr. Brightman, in
J.T.S. for Jan., 1928, p. 159) and should be translated
not " and then from this place," but " and so, after
that."

[2] *Apol. c. Ar.* § 35.
[3] Socr., *H.E.* II. xvii. § 7.
[4] Soz., *H.E.* III. x. § 1.
[5] *Ep.* xiv. § 12.
[6] *Decr. Ps.-Isid.*, 459: ed. F. Hinschius.

dence of that sole and supreme jurisdiction ascribed to his see in later times.

The Dedication Council of Antioch,[1] in the summer of 341, was the answer to Pope Julius. Constantius himself was present,[2] and the Council though for the most part consisting of conservatives in theology, was so far dominated by an Eusebian minority as to re-affirm the decision of Tyre against Athanasius by decreeing that, " if a bishop accused of certain offences has been tried by the bishops of the province and all have unanimously given sentence against him, he may not be tried again by others but the unanimous decision of the bishops of the province must hold good."[3] The West, however, meant to provide for such cases by a gradation of courts, under the direction of the Roman see; and the Emperor Constans pressed upon his brother a demand for a General Council,[4] with this end in view. Constantius was in no position to refuse, for he was face to face with a renewal of the Persian Wars and Constans was master of two-thirds of the Empire. Accordingly the Council met at Sardica, now Sofia, July, 343, a city just within the borders of the Western Empire, and so under the protection of Constans. The Sardican prelates sometimes addressed the Pope as " our dearest brother " or " most beloved brother " and sometimes wrote to him as to " their head, *i.e.* to the see of the apostle Peter,"[5] for this was a Western

---

[1] Mirbt[4], No. 123.
[2] Ath., *de Syn.* § 25.
[3] Canon 15: Hefele, *Councils* i. 71.
[4] Ath., *Apol. ad. Const.* § 4.
[5] Hilary, *Fragment* ii. § 9.

Council, and the Pope was admittedly head of Western Christendom. They beg him to communicate their decisions to " our brethren of Sicily, Sardinia and Italy," *i.e.* to the provinces more directly under his control. They also let it be obvious that not the " head " but the Emperors had summoned the Council, and even determined its programme.[1] All this was as usual, at that date. But among their decisions was something new.

The Council of Sardica, in two canons,[2] offered to a bishop condemned by his colleagues the opportunity of reconsideration under the direction of the Roman see. " The two canons are not easy to unravel. On the whole, it would seem that the provisions of the former canon are more general and include, even if they have not specially in view, a less serious class of cases, such as disputes between two bishops; while the latter applies only to actual trial and deposition and defines the machinery of appeal more minutely. In the first case, if the defeated bishop claims a re-hearing, then either the bishops who have acted as judges or the bishops of a neighbouring province (not apparently the unsuccessful litigant himself) may refer to the bishop of Rome, ' in honour of the memory of St. Peter,' the question whether the trial ought to be reheard and, if so, who were to rehear it; the judges in the latter case are apparently to be selected by the Pope from among the local bishops. But, in the second and fuller series

---

[1] Hilary, *Fragment* ii. § 11.

[2] Canons III and VII, as in the revised text of C. H. Turner, *J.T.S.* for April 1902: (vol. iii., pp. 693 sq.): *Doc. Ch. Hist.* ii., No. 19.

of prescriptions, the right of appeal is given direct to any bishop deposed after trial by bishops of ' the region.' The Roman bishop has to decide (a) as before, whether the case is to be reheard at all, and (b) if it is, whether the bishops of the next province (to that from which the appeal comes) will suffice to decide the case, or whether the assistance of a presbyter-legate from Rome will be desirable."[1]

In estimating the nature and extent of the powers so conveyed, three points are to be noted. (a) They are new, for they were devised to meet a particular occasion, viz. the case of a bishop wrongfully deposed. (b) They are limited, and not absolute. " In neither class of cases is there any provision for the Pope's calling up the business into his own court and exercising personal jurisdiction."[2] What he acquired was not a right of appeal, but a right of revision. (c) They were not inherent, but conferred by vote of the Council. " Osius episcopus dixit . . . Si hoc omnibus placet ? Synodus respondit: Placet "—" Si ergo et hoc vobis placet ? Universi dixerunt: Placet et constituatur." There was indeed a clause: " Si vobis placet, sanctissimi Petri apostoli memoriam honoremus." But such language as this was merely common form; and had there been an appellate jurisdiction already in the Roman see, the language of the canon would have been different. Nevertheless, the Papacy stood to gain by this grant at Sardica. For whereas hitherto " the special authority of the Church of Rome was

---

[1] Turner, *J.T.S.* for April 1902 (vol. iii., p. 388).
[2] *Ib.*

felt rather than defined,"[1] its powers were now given legal recognition, though by definition limited to particular cases and to certain modes of exercise.

§ 4. The episcopate of Pope Liberius, 352-†66, marks the recovery of its prestige by the Roman see in conflict with the Cæsaropapism of Constantius, very much as did the pontificate of Pius VII, 1800-†23 in the conflict with Napoleon. Julius was fortunate in having the civil power at his back. Liberius had it against him. His episcopate covers the period of the sole supremacy of Constantius, 351-†61, when, free from the Persian Wars and victorious over the usurper Magnentius, he was free to devote himself to the support of the Arianizers. He successfully intimidated the Westerns at the Councils of Arles, 353, and Milan, 355. But there were great prelates left in possession of their sees who treated his *protégés* as heretics—Liberius, Hosius, Hilary and Athanasius. These had to be won over, or got rid of; and the Emperor began with Liberius. He sent a eunuch to Rome who tried him with bribes and threats; but had to report that the Pope would yield only to force. Liberius was then taken to Milan, there to confront the Emperor himself.[2] In vain, and the Pope was banished, 355, to Berœa in Thrace,[3] in the hope that lonely confinement might shake his resolution. It had its effect, for, " lacking endurance to the end,"[4] he gave way, and was allowed

[1] L. Duchesne, *Early History of the Church*, i. 390.
[2] Ath., *Hist. Ar.* §§ 35-9.
[3] Thdt., *H.E.*, II. xvi. § 27.
[4] Ath., *Apol. c. Ar.*, § 89.

to return to Rome, 2nd Aug., 358. Of his fall and recovery there is no doubt. " Liberius tædio victus exilii, in hæreticam pravitatem subscribens, Romam quasi victor intravit."[1] While he was absent, the ultra-Arians, at the Council of Sirmium, 357, put forth the creed known as " The Blasphemy ";[2] and so revealed themselves in their true colours. The effect was to alarm their *quondam* allies among the conservatives, and so to turn them towards the Nicenes; but not till after further defections at the Council of Ariminum (now Rimini) 359, under pressure from Constantius. Then the process of recovery set in, but the initiative did not lie with the Pope. It was the work of Athanasius, Hilary of Poitiers, and Eusebius of Vercelli, and Liberius followed up their efforts by a letter, 363, to the bishops of Italy who had compromised themselves at Ariminum. Here he urged them to clear themselves. " Repentance," he writes, as if with an eye to his own past, " effaces the fault of inexperience."[3] Then it fell to him, as a true successor of Peter in character, if not in office, " when he was converted to strengthen his brethren "; for he had the felicity of receiving into Catholic communion a deputation of Semi-Arians from the East. They handed to " their lord and brother and fellow-minister Liberius " a written formulary,[4] accepting the Nicene Creed. Thereupon the Pope admitted them to communion,

---

[1] Jerome, *Chron. ad ann.* 352: Mirbt[4], No. 124.
[2] Hilary, *De synodis*, § 11: *Doc. Ch. Hist.* ii., No. 25.
[3] *Imperitiæ culpam*: Hilary, *Fragment*, xii. §§ 1-2: Jaffé, No. 223.
[4] Socr., *H.E.* IV. xii. §§ 9-20.

and sent a letter to those who had accredited them—
sixty-four bishops in all—accepting their advances,[1]
as from " Liberius episcopus Italiæ et omnes Occi-
dentis episcopi." In this correspondence we note that
the appeal was made not to the Pope alone but to the
Pope as representing the West: that its object was to
gain the protection of the Emperor Valentinian I
against his brother, the Arian persecutor Valens, and
that the East was more concerned about this than about
the prerogative of the Roman see or the unity of the
Church. Athanasius, at this period, is the leader,
not the bishop of Rome, of which he speaks as " an
apostolic see " and the metropolis of " Romania,"[2]
by contrast with Milan as the metropolis of " Italy."[3]
Nevertheless, though but one among bishops of several
such sees in Eastern eyes, and that under the conditions
of the moment not the most prominent, Liberius had
recovered for the Roman see its prestige. He was
master of the West and its representative in all dealings
with the East; and, while he left it to the Emperor to
convoke Councils, it was for him to be judge in matters
of faith.

[1] Socr., *H.E* IV. xii. §§ 21-37 = *Optatissimum nobis*: Jaffé,
No. 228.
[2] Ath., *Hist. Ar.* § 35.
[3] *Ib.* § 33.

CHAPTER VI

DAMASUS

THE episcopate of Damasus is a landmark in the history of the Roman primacy. For the wealth of his see, the support which he received from the State, and the claim that he vindicated for his see in reply to its rival at Constantinople, gave to it a pre-eminence both new and lasting.

§ 1. The wealth of the Roman see was due to the devotion of the ladies of Roman society to their bishop. They had come, in all their finery, for an audience with Constantius, and so persuaded him to restore Liberius to his see. The see thus became a prize worth fighting for, and, on the death of Liberius, 24th Sept. 366, the faction-fights, which had disgraced his election, broke out again. The majority elected Damasus that very day in the church of San Lorenzo in Lucina, but put off his consecration till 1st Oct. in St. John Lateran. The minority assembled in the Julian basilica, now Santa Maria in Trastevere for the election of Ursinus, also on 24th Sept., and had him consecrated there and then. A month of rioting ensued till 26th Oct. when the partisans of Damasus attacked the followers of Ursinus in the basilica of Liberius, now Santa Maria Maggiore, and left one hundred and thirty-seven dead in the church.[1] It is difficult to

[1] Ammianus Marcellinus, *Res Gestæ* XXVII. iii. §§ 12, 13: *Doc. Ch. Hist.* ii. No. 94.

distribute the blame, or to bring it home personally to Damasus. Both parties must be held responsible for the bloodshed, for " Damasus and Ursinus were both immoderately eager to obtain the bishopric ";[1] an eagerness which the pagan but not unfriendly historian and contemporary goes on to account for by a picture of the wealth and secularity of the Roman see.[2]

§ 2. The rights of the election were assigned to Damasus, but his rival, after an interval of banishment, avenged himself in the courts of law. About 370, he instituted a criminal suit, appearing as accuser himself, and, in a second suit, after the accession of the Emperor Gratian, 375-†83, he made further charges against the Pope before the Vicarius Urbis through one Isaac, a converted Jew. But Gratian took the case into his own hands; banished the accusers, Isaac to Spain, and Ursinus to Cologne, and cleared the Pope of the calumnies against him. Damasus was not satisfied. He knew how to rely on the secular arm. But he wished to have his innocence attested in an ecclesiastical assembly. Accordingly a Council met in Rome in May and June, 382, and probably the sixth under Damasus;[3] and presented a petition to Gratian, beginning *Et hoc Gloriæ Vestræ*,[4] in which they make two important requests.

The first, §§ 1-9, has reference to Ursinus, and asks that, the Government having restored order by banishing the disturbers of the peace, the Emperor should

---

[1] *Ib.* § 12. [2] *Ib.* §§ 14-15.
[3] Puller, *Prim. Saints*[3], 542 sq.
[4] Migne, *P.L.* xiii. 575-84: *Doc. Ch. Hist.* ii., No. 58.

confirm the privilege,[1] previously acknowledged, of
the bishop of Rome and his fellows to try the cases of
bishops still recalcitrant, so that no bishop might be
brought before a secular judge.[2] Let him order that
such offenders, if living in Italy, should be compelled
to appear in Rome; if farther off, before the local
metropolitan; if metropolitans themselves, either in
Rome, or before judges appointed by the bishop of
Rome. The see of Rome would thus acquire a widely
extended authority in cases of first instance. But let
provision also be made for its intervention in appeals.
Any bishop who had been condemned, and had doubts
about the fairness of his metropolitan or other episcopal
judges, should be allowed the right of appeal either
to the bishop of Rome, or to a synod of, at least, fifteen
neighbouring bishops.

A second request, §§ 10-11, looked back to the indignity heaped upon Damasus by Isaac in summoning
the Pope before the ordinary courts. The bishop of
Rome should be sheltered from such calumniators:
and any cases to which he was party, if not committed
to his Council, should be heard by the Emperor in
person.

Gratian replied with the rescript *Ordinariorum
sententiæ*,[3] addressed to Anulinus, Vicarius Urbis,
378-9, *i.e.* to the official who, as the immediate subor-
dinate of the Prætorian Prefect of Italy, governed the
suburbicarian provinces. The Emperor begins by
remarking, § 1, that, if his letters to Simplicius, pre-

---

[1] *Et hoc*, etc. §§ 1, 4.   [2] *Ib.* § 2.
[3] *P.L.* xiii. 583-8.

decessor of Anulinus, in 374, had not been ignored, Ursinus and other disturbers of the peace, §§ 2-3, would by this time have disappeared. The innocence of Damasus, § 4, had been vindicated by Valentinian: and, § 5, they must be sent off at once.

Then, as to the two requests of the Roman Synod. In § 6,[1] he adopts its distinction between bishops of the suburbicarian provinces, where the Pope was sole metropolitan, and bishops who live in " the more distant regions " of the Western Empire. He orders that the former are to be tried either at Rome or by synods elsewhere (such as were usual in Sicily[2] and, perhaps, in Sardinia and Corsica): but that the latter— bishops, that is, of Africa, Spain, North Italy and Gaul—when under accusation, are to be remitted by the local magistrate to the court of the metropolitan. So far, the rescript dealt with suits of first instance in the case of ordinary bishops: and there was no enlargement of papal powers. But, in the case of metropolitans, and by way of appeal, Gratian proceeds to confer two new powers on the Roman see. " The Pope was made master of the judicial process by which all accused metropolitans throughout the West were to be tried. He might either have them summoned to Rome to be tried there, or he might appoint judges by whom they would have to be tried elsewhere. And, in the second place, ordinary bishops throughout the Western Empire, who had been tried in the first instance away from Rome by the provincial synod or

---

[1] Mirbt[4], No. 133: *Doc. Ch. Hist.* ii., No. 65.
[2] Ath., *Ad. Afros*, § 1.

by some local synod of bishops, might, if they chose,
appeal either to the Pope, or to a synod of fifteen bishops
having sees in the neighbourhood."[1]   This was a great
step forward in the growth of papal authority; but it
was no recognition of inherent rights.   On the contrary
the new jurisdiction was both erected and annexed to
the Roman see by the civil power, which was thus
very complaisant to Damasus and to the first request
of his Council that bishops should be tried by their
fellow-bishops and by the Pope in particular.   The
second, that the bishop of Rome himself should be
saved from the indignity of appearing before the
ordinary courts, was quietly refused.   Gratian confined
himself to directing, § 7, that, where the accusers were
known to be persons of doubtful morals or mere
calumniators, their evidence should not be admitted.[2]

Such was the supremacy over the West now conceded
by the State to the Roman see; but " ecclesiastically
the new legislation, so far as it applied to countries
outside Italy, was null and void."[3]   The relations
between Rome and the East were of a different kind;
and led to the adoption of a theory by Damasus and
his successors calculated to afford a *religious* basis for
the new authority thus acquired.

§ 3. Basil was archbishop of Cæsarea in Cappadocia,
370-†9, during the episcopate of Damasus at Rome.
He was harassed by the persecution of the Emperor
Valens, 364-†78; depressed by the desolation of the

[1] F. W. Puller, *Primitive Saints and the See of Rome*[3], 151.
[2] *P.L.* xiii. 588.
[3] Puller, *op. cit.*, 155: *cf.* Batiffol, *Le siège apostolique*,
47 sqq.

churches " from Illyricum to Egypt,"[1] whose condition
he likens to a sea-fight in which all is confusion;[2]
and anxious to heal the divisions at Antioch, where
the allegiance of Catholics was divided between a
majority which acknowledged Meletius and a minority
which held tenaciously to Paulinus as bishop. Basil
and the East supported Meletius: but to Damasus at
Rome and Athanasius at Alexandria the legitimate
bishop was Paulinus. To Basil, Athanasius was the
natural mediator between East and West;[3] but he died
before he could be got to intervene. Meanwhile
Basil looked for a remedy to assistance from the West;
and between 371-7 he sent missions—four in all—with
urgent appeals for help; and, in particular, for a deputation in force of Western bishops to visit and shew
sympathy with the East. He made a special appeal to
Damasus;[4] but, as time went on, he found that all
his efforts were but coldly received and nothing was
done. His tone changes: and, while it is noticeable
that with the exception of his one letter to Damasus,
his letters are addressed to " The bishops of the West "[5]
or " To his fellow-ministers in Italy and Gaul "[6] in
singular disregard of their " coryphæus " at Rome whom
he thought half a heretic for his support of Marcellus,[7]
he eventually came to use such language of the Pope as
would be inconceivable if he had been aware of any
obligation to the paramount authority of the Roman
see. Some of it may be accounted for by " my old

---

[1] *Ep*. lxx. [2] *De Spiritu Sancto*, § 76.
[3] *Epp*. lxvi.: lxix. § 1. [4] *Ep*. lxx.
[5] *Epp*. xc.: ccxlii. [6] *Epp*. xcii.: ccxliii.
[7] *Ep*. ccxxxix. § 2: *cf* lxix. § 2.

plague, the liver ":[1] but it is too common with him not
to be deliberate. Thus he says that a letter of his
was " not very welcome to the preciser sort (Damasus)
at Rome ";[2] that the Pope is "a man proud, exalted
and sitting up aloft, and so quite incapable of listening
to those who tell him the truth from down below, like
my poor brother Gregory [of Nyssa] ";[3] that he is
" totally ignorant of what is going on here;"[4] and that
" no help is to be expected from Western supercilious-
ness."[5]   As to the case of rival bishops at Antioch,
Basil writes: " I congratulate those (Paulinus) who
have received letters from Rome (assigning them the
episcopate of the church there) . . . But I shall never
be able to persuade myself on these grounds to ignore
Meletius . . . I shall never consent to give in, merely
because somebody (Paulinus) is very much elated at
having received a letter from men (Damasus)."[6]   The
attitude of Basil towards Rome was, in short, a mixture
" of deference and disdain."   Like other Easterns,
he made little of the prerogatives of the Roman see,
except when he wanted its assistance; and its primacy,
though not repudiated, counted with him for little.

§ 4. The Council of Constantinople, May to July,
381, was less disdainful and did not forget the Roman
Primacy.

Shortly after the death of St. Basil, 1st Jan., 379, his
friend Gregory of Nazianzus arrived in Constantinople
to inaugurate the Catholic revival there.   It   was

---

[1] *Ep*. cxxxviii. § 1.   [2] *Ib*. § 2.
[3] *Ep*. ccxv.   [4] *Ep*. ccxiv. § 2.
[5] *Ep*. ccxxxix. § 2.   [6] *Ep*. ccxiv. § 2.

aided by the accession, 19th Jan., of Theodosius as Emperor, 379-†95. He was an ardent Catholic, and the founder also of the Orthodox State. The Easterns, sensitive as ever to the way in which the wind was blowing from the Court, adhered at a Synod of Antioch, Sept.-Oct., 379, to the Roman Synod of 369, and tried in vain to reconcile the division between Meletius and Paulinus in that city. Damasus acknowledged their deference to the Apostolic See, and reminded them both of its prerogative and of its source in the Apostle St. Peter—writing as from " the holy church in which the Apostle sat and taught us . . . how we ought to handle the helm which has been entrusted to us."[1] Theodosius, meanwhile, lay ill at Thessalonica. But on his recovery, and before he set out for his campaign against the Goths, he was baptized by Acholius, its bishop and papal Vicar of Eastern Illyricum, recently assigned to the dominions of Theodosius. He then put out the edict *Cunctos populos*,[2] 27th Feb., 380, in order to distinguish between Catholic and Heretic, and to let the latter know what they might expect. " It is our pleasure," he says, " that all the peoples who are governed by our Clemency should steadfastly adhere to the religion which was taught by St. Peter to the Romans, which faithful tradition has preserved, and which is now professed by the pontiff Damasus and by Peter, bishop of Alexandria, a man of apostolic holiness . . . We authorize the followers of this doctrine to assume the title of Catholic Christians . . . ":

[1] Damasus, *Ep.* vii. (*P.L.* xiii. 370): Thdt., *H.E.* V. x. § 1.
[2] Mirbt[4], No. 134: *Doc. Ch. Hist.* ii., No. 69.

their centres of communion, presumably for West and East respectively, being thus not Rome only, but Alexandria as well. This done, the Emperor set out for the Gothic War. He returned victorious: and, 14th Nov., he entered Constantinople in triumph, to take up the settlement of religion in his part of the Empire.

Three questions awaited him here: the Arian and other heresies: the succession to the see of Constantinople: and the rivalries at Antioch.

As to heresy, Theodosius lost no time in giving effect to the warnings of his previous edict by *Nullus hæreticis*,[1] of 10th Jan., 381: which banished all heretics from the churches. In respect of the see of Constantinople, he had already provided for it by appointing Gregory of Nazianzus to be bishop, 26th Nov., 380: but the situation was presently complicated by the attempt of Maximus, an adventurer from Egypt, to gain possession of the see. In regard to Antioch, Sapor, a General sent by Theodosius, early in Feb., 381, to enforce *Nullus hæreticis*, manifested an excess of zeal in not only assigning the churches to Meletius but in extruding Paulinus, who was no heretic but the rightful bishop in the eyes of Alexandria and Rome.

The situation thus called for further action; and, at the prayer of Ulphilas, bishop of the Goths, 341-†81, well-known at Constantinople and himself an Arian,[2] the Emperor summoned the Council of Constantinople:

---

[1] Mirbt[4], No. 181.
[2] See his creed in Hahn, *Symbole*[3], § 196: and *Doc. Ch. Hist.* ii., No. 70.

which, from 514-9, when it was recognized by Pope Hormisdas,[1] began to take rank as the Second Œcumenical Council. It met in May, with Meletius as president—a purely Eastern Council to deal with Eastern affairs. It failed to rally the Macedonians, but condemned them with all other heretics.[2] It declared the ordination of Maximus null and void:[3] and, on the death of Meletius in June, enthroned Gregory as bishop of Constantinople. Then, in order to prevent for the future such invasion of one bishop's territory by another, it reaffirmed[4] the Nicene legislation[5] that the great sees—Alexandria, Antioch and others— should observe their existing limits of jurisdiction. As a corollary to this, and to secure for Constantinople a status which should render it unassailable in the East by giving it rank above Alexandria, the Council ordained that " the bishop of Constantinople should have the primacy of honour next after the bishop of Rome, because it is new Rome."[6] Finally, in spite of the compact made, Feb., 381, between Meletius and Paulinus that on the death of either of them the survivor should be accepted as bishop of Antioch, the Council appointed Flavian to that see. Gregory, who, for the sake of peace, had urged the keeping of the compact, resigned both his see and the presidency of the Council; and the Emperor appointed Nectarius, who succeeded him in both capacities. On the request of the Council, he gave confirmation to its proceedings:[7] and by *Epis-*

---

[1] F. W. Puller, *Prim. Saints*[3], 360. [2] Canon 1.
[3] Canon 4. [4] Canon 2. [5] Canons 4, 6.
[6] Canon 3: Mirbt[4], No. 137: *Doc. Ch. Hist.* ii., No. 71.
[7] Sozomen, *H.E.* VII. ix. § 5.

copis tradi of 30th July, he enumerated certain bishops
of the chief sees of the East whom he would recognize
as centres of communion. No mention was made of
Damasus, as the Council was not concerned with the
West; nor of Flavian of Antioch, because he was not
yet consecrated.

We may now finish the story, in order to appreciate
its bearing on the Roman primacy.

§ 5. The ink of the Imperial confirmation was
scarcely dry when, late in 381, two synods were held
in the north of Italy, at Aquileia in September and at
Milan in December, both under the influence of St.
Ambrose. His letters[1] are the authority for what
happened, especially in regard to the disputed successions at Antioch and Constantinople, where East and
West, after what took place at the Council of Constantinople, were on different sides.

At Aquileia, in a letter to Theodosius, the bishops
pronounced for Paulinus at Antioch,[2] and begged him
to order a General Council at Alexandria to discuss
" with whom communion is to be maintained." They
seem to have been unaware, as yet, of what had been
done at Constantinople in this matter.

At Milan, however, three months later, they appear
to have heard of what had been done there for the
settlement of the successions both in the Eastern
capital and at Antioch. They regret in their synodal
letter to Theodosius[3] that, in spite of the compact
between Meletius and Paulinus, Flavian had been

---

[1] *Epp.* viii.-xiv.   [2] *Ep.* xii. § 4.
[3] *Ep.* xiii.

appointed to Antioch:[1] the more so as this was done, they believe, on the advice of Nectarius, the regularity of whose consecration they consider uncertain.[2] Maximus, it would seem, had arrived in Milan soon after Easter, 381, and had successfully imposed upon a Council held there about the end of May:[3] at least, so far as to induce it to accept his episcopal status and to write to Theodosius in his favour. Now they write again, threatening to break off all relations with the East unless Maximus is reinstated, or unless the East will agree that the whole matter shall be referred to a General Council to meet in Rome.[4] Theodosius sent them " an august and princely answer,"[5] which has not come down to us; but it told them the truth about the pretensions of Maximus, and maintained the Eastern view in favour of Flavian. So we gather from another letter[6] sent to Theodosius in reply, by a further synod held at Milan shortly after Easter, 17th April, 382. They were not satisfied, and it was only when they went to Rome for the sixth of the Damasine synods, in May or June, 382, that they were undeceived. Damasus had been informed, by Acholius of Thessalonica, perhaps as early as the year 380, of the baseless nature of the claims of Maximus. They dropped that worthy at last, but continued to support Paulinus, and did not relax their pressure on Gratian for a General Council. He acquiesced, and summoned it to meet in Rome.[7] But he reckoned without his colleague; for Theodosius

[1] *Ep.* xiii. § 2.   [2] *Ib.* § 3.
[3] Concilium nuper, *ib.* § 3.   [4] *Ib.* § 6.
[5] *Ep.* xiv. § 4.   [6] *Ep.* xiv.
[7] Soz., *H.E.* VII. xi. § 4: Thdt., *H.E.* V. ix. § 8.

disregarded the theory of Ambrose that the affairs of the East were not to be settled without the consent of the West:[1] and preferred a Council under his own eye. Accordingly the year 382 was marked by two synods: one at Constantinople in the summer, and the other in the autumn at Rome.

At Constantinople the prelates, much the same as those of the Second General Council, in their synodal letter to the West,[2] excused themselves from going thither[3] and preferred Constantinople as it was nearer home.[4] They affirmed their adherence to the Nicene Faith;[5] and then, turning to the contested successions at Constantinople and Antioch, by appeal to the Nicene rule, as they call it, which prescribes that bishops shall be consecrated by their comprovincials, with the aid, if necessary, of neighbouring bishops,[6] they seek to justify the appointments of Nectarius[7] and Flavian.[8] This was a polite way of telling the Westerns that the promotions in question were no concern of theirs; but they asked, and apparently expected, their consent.[9]

§ 6. The Roman Synod, to which this letter was addressed, was the seventh held under Pope Damasus. Ambrose was there,[10] but he was ill, and took little part;[11] Acholius who, though his country was now part of the Eastern Empire, was papal Vicar and ranked

---

[1] *Ep.* xiii. § 4.
[2] Thdt., *H.E.* V. ix.
[3] *Ib.* § 8.
[4] *Ib.* § 9.
[5] *Ib.* §§ 10-12.
[6] *Ib.* § 14.
[7] *Ib.* § 15.
[8] *Ib.* § 16.
[9] *Ib.* §§ 17, 18.
[10] Thdt., *H.E.* V. ix. § 1.
[11] *Ep.* xv. § 10.

with the Westerns; and the delegates sent from the recent Council of Constantinople.[1] They excommunicated Flavian: but they appear to have been too well aware of the record of Maximus to interfere with Nectarius. Instead, they put out a document[2] of great importance in the development of the Roman primacy. Though it is held by some to be " of the second half of the fifth century " and no " Roman " document[3] and by others to be " no papal ordinance but the production of an anonymous scholar of the sixth century probably in Italy,"[4] it has been assigned with greater probability to " the Roman Council under Damasus " of 382.[5] " The document contains . . . the first official definition of papal claims. Roman primacy (' cæteris ecclesiis prælata,' ' primatum obtinuit ') is grounded with obvious reference to the vote of the Council in 381 in favour of Constantinople ' on no synodal decisions,' but directly on the promise of Christ to Peter recorded in the Gospel. Respect for Roman tradition imposes next a mention of ' the fellowship of the most blessed Paul '; but the dominant *motif* reappears in the concluding paragraph, and the three sees whose prerogative was recognized at Nicæa are transformed into a Petrine hierarchy with its

[1] Thdt., *H.E.* V. ix. § 9.
[2] Known as the *Decretum Gelasianum :* see Mirbt[4], No. 191.
[3] Batiffol, *Le siège apostolique*, 149 sq.
[4] *J.T.S.* xiv. 471.
[5] C. H. Turner in *J.T.S.* i. 554 sqq., with text, 560: and in the *Cambridge Mediæval History*, i. 173; Dom Chapman, O.S.B., *Studies in the Early Papacy*, i. 20 n. 2: and Erich Caspar, *Geschichte des Papsttums*, i. 247, 598 sq.

' prima sedes ' at Rome, its ' secunda sedes ' at Alexandria, and its ' tertia sedes ' at Antioch."[1]

It is easy to account for the rise of this theory. It was prompted by a reaction against the ambition of the upstart see of Constantinople, as also by the fear (not without justification by later events) that the unity of the Church, hitherto protected by regard for " the Roman Church " as " the head of the Roman world,"[2] would be imperilled by the growing divergence between East and West. But its foundations, whether in Scripture or in history, were insecure. The text, Matt. xvi. 18, 19, is capable of more than one interpretation: while, in point of fact, the pre-eminence of the Roman see was due in part, though not entirely, as the Easterns maintained,[3] to the civil greatness of the city, but also to its being the only Apostolic see in the West, and the only church in Christendom with two Apostles, and the two chief among the Apostles, for its founders. Peter, moreover, was not the first bishop of Rome, but Linus: and the stages of his sole association with the see are clearly marked. First, in the

---

[1] *C.M.H.* i. 173.

[2] Ambrose, *Ep.* xi. § 4. " As regards the position of the See of Peter, Ambrose certainly entertained a profound veneration for the Roman Church, particularly as the consistent upholder of the Christian faith in all its purity and integrity. In that Church the Creed of the Apostles had been preserved undefiled (*Ep.* xlii. § 5): to be in communion with that Church was a guarantee of correct faith (*Ep.* xi. § 4). . . . He does not, however, anywhere ascribe to the Roman pontiff supreme jurisdiction over the whole Church, or recognize him as the final and sovereign interpreter of the laws of ecclesiastical discipline " (F. H. Dudden, *The Life and Times of S. Ambrose*, ii. 641 sq.)

[3] CP. 3: Chalc. 28.

opening of the third century when " the habit grew up of including the name of the Apostle-founder as the first of the list [*sc.* of local bishops] rather than as a title at the head of it . . . Hippolytus being the earliest writer in whom we can detect the novel method of reckoning."[1] Next, in the writings of St. Cyprian, who was " the first writer to talk of ' The Chair of Peter ' only."[2] Third, in the use first made of Matt. xvi. 18, 19 by Pope Stephen to claim a Petrine authority. And, finally, in the theory as set forth by the Council under Damasus.

But the theory itself is open to further objection. The original order of the great sees, as recognized by the Council of Nicæa,[3] is Rome, Alexandria, Antioch: these being the first three cities of the Empire, in that order. But, if they were all to be reckoned as Petrine sees—Peter having been bishop first of Antioch then of Rome, and Mark, his disciple, founder of the church of Alexandria—what justification is there, it may be asked, for putting Alexandria, the see of the disciple, before Antioch, the see of the Apostle himself ? Nevertheless, such was the disregard both of Scripture and of history required by the tradition long established at Rome of derivation from Peter only, that the theory was not only accepted at Rome by the Council of Damasus in view of current dangers, but so taken for granted by his successors that it ruled the thought and language of the Popes from Damasus onwards, until it was

---

[1] C. H. Turner, *Catholic and Apostolic*, 225.
[2] The same, in *C.M.H.* i. 17.
[3] Nic. 6

rounded off in still more explicit and imperative form by St. Leo. " Under the pontificate of Pope Damasus a long step forward was " thus " taken in formulating the claim of the Roman Church to be the exclusive inheritor of all and more than all that the New Testament tells us of the prerogative of St. Peter."[1]

[1] Turner, *Catholic and Apostolic*, 233.

CHAPTER VII

ROME AND AFRICA

SEVEN Popes ruled from the death of Damasus to the accession of Leo. They were Siricius †399; Anastasius †401; Innocent I †417; Zosimus †418; Boniface †422; Cœlestine †432; and Sixtus III †440; We must now see what use they made of the primacy, and with what success.

§ 1. Among the letters of Siricius, 384-†99, four bear upon his authority. It extends over Spain, Illyria, Italy and Africa.

In *Directa ad decessorem*,[1] the decretal epistle of 10th Feb., 385, addressed to Himerius, bishop of Tarragona, the Pope finds himself consulted on questions of discipline and gives his rulings. " We refuse not," he writes, § 1, " to reply point by point to your enquiries, and to give such answers as we owe to the inspiration of our Lord. Our office does not permit us either to shut our eyes or to hold our tongue. Beyond all others we must have a zeal for the Christian religion. We bear the burden of all who are in difficulties: or rather he who bears the burden in us is the blessed Apostle St. Peter who in everything, as we trust, protects and watches over us, the heirs of his administration."

---

[1] *Ep.* i (*P.L.* xiii. 1132 sqq.): Mirbt⁴, No. 139: Jaffé, No. 255.

Siricius then proceeds to deal with the questions submitted to him and, § 20, concludes:[1] " In each case on which, in answer to the report[2] which you have made (*relatisti*) to the Roman church as to the head of the body to which you belong, we have now given, as we believe, sufficient replies (*responsa*). We urge you so to observe the canons and decrees (*decretalia*) as to let our reply (*rescripsimus*) be known not only to your own ' diocese ' (Tarraconensis) but to all our colleagues throughout [the ' dioceses ' of] Carthagena, Bætica, Lusitania, Gallæcia, and the neighbouring provinces. No bishop is at liberty to ignore the decisions of the Apostolic See, or the venerable decrees of the canons." Siricius, in short, writes as having the authority of St. Peter living and acting in his successor: so the theory of the papacy is taking shape. But, as yet, that authority scarcely extends further than to see that the canons are observed, except that his decretals rank as on the same level with them, for the pope is master of the West.

Similar powers are assumed in two letters of 386:

[1] *Doc. Ch. Hist.* ii., No. 75.

[2] For " le valeur juridique des termes *relatio, rescriptum* " see quotations in Batiffol, *Le catholicisme de S. Augustin* 404 n. 3. " Le terme de *relatio* designait les rapports que les functionnaires provinciaux envoyaient à l'empereur pour obtenir de lui, sur les points juridiques douteux, les *réscrits* ou *réponses* qui étaient alors la forme la plus commune des lois imperiales. *Rescripta* ou *responsa reddere* était, dans la langue officielle, l'expression qui s'appliquait à l'envoi de ces décisions souveraines "—another instance of the debt of the papacy to the State. Further, note the distinction between a *Rescript* and an *Edict*. " Les *réscrits* ne sont pas des actes qui créent le droit, comme font les *édits*, mais qui interprètent le droit ": *ib.* 403.

in *Cum in unum*[1] and *Cogitantibus nobis*.[2]   Addressed
originally to the bishops of the Vicariate of Rome, they
both were sent on further afield: the former to the
bishops of Africa and the latter to the " Orthodox
[bishops] of the different provinces " [of the West].
They testify to the authority of the Roman see at this
date as extending throughout the Latin Church.
Cum in unum emanates, § 1, from the Roman Synod
" assembled together " under Siricius " at the relics
of the holy Apostle Peter "—guarantees, it would seem,
of Peter still ruling in his see—" from whom both
apostolate and episcopate in Christ took their beginning ": and lays it down, § 2, " that no bishop should
dare to ordain without the knowledge [in the suburbicarian churches, or Vicariate of Rome] of the Apostolic
See or [in Africa] of the Primate " under penalty,
§ 4, " of excommunication and the pains of hell."
In *Cogitantibus nobis* the Pope writes, § 1, that " he
must raise his voice, for as the care of all the churches
[2 Cor. xi. 28, a phrase appropriated to himself from
St. Paul] is committed to him, he can but expect the
judgment of God if he keeps silence."   It is hardly
necessary to mention *Etiam dudum*,[3] for it merely
renews to Anysius, bishop of Thessalonica, the office
of papal Vicar in Illyria, bestowed on him and his
predecessors by previous popes.

We may thus proceed to a summary of the situation
c. 400, so far as it exhibits the stage of development

---

[1] *Ep.* v. (*P.L.* xiii. 1155-62): Jaffé, No. 258.
[2] *Ep.* vi. (*P.L.* xiii. 1164-8): Jaffé, No. 263.
[3] *Ep.* iv. (*P.L.* xiii. 1149): Mirbt[4], No. 140: Jaffé, No. 259.

reached under Siricius and Anastasius, 399-†401.
Both have a place above the episcopate. It is not
contested; though it appears to be that, only as one
among other great bishops. Anastasius, " informed "
by Theophilus, bishop of Alexandria, " intimated " to
Simplicianus, bishop of Milan, that he had rejected
and condemned " everything written in former days
by Origen that is contrary to our faith."[1] But it is
limited; for the East goes on its own way and does not
mind if out of communion with the West, as in the
case of Flavian, bishop of Antioch, 381-†98. Rome
is treated as a particular church, one among many,
as by Rufinus. " I declare," he writes to Pope Anastasius, " in Christ's name that I never held any other
faith but . . . the faith which is held by the church
of Rome, by that of Alexandria, and by my own church
of Aquileia: and which is also preached at Jerusalem."[2]
Africa still appeals to " ecclesiæ transmarinæ ": not
to Rome alone, but to Rome and Milan. By A.D. 400
East and West are reunited. Rome governs the ten
churches of the Vicariate of Rome, together with
Illyricum, the seven provinces of the Vicariate of Italy
at this date belonging to Milan and Aquileia: though,
before Milan and Aquileia came into existence—i.e., at
the time of the Council of Nicæa—the sphere of Rome
was Italy as a whole. But Milan, about 400, was on
the wane: and Rome on the way to an authority co-
extensive with the Empire of the West.

[1] Jerome, *Ep.* xcv. § 2 (*P.L.* xxii. 774). *Doc. Ch. Hist.*,
No. 114.
[2] *Apol. ad Anast.* § 8.

§ 2. During the episcopate of Innocent I, 402-†17, with the retirement of Honorius to Ravenna and the capture of Rome by Alaric, " there could be no question that, from this time, the greatest man in Rome was the Pope."[1] His letters reveal both the extent of his authority and the view which he held of its source. In the West it was generally acknowledged: but with some qualification in Africa. In the East it was exerted and welcomed in defence of St. Chrysostom, but directed to secure the decision in his case by reference to the principles laid down at Nicæa.

Since the incorporation of Eastern Illyricum into the Eastern Empire, 379, when Gratian entrusted it to Theodosius, there was a natural tendency for these regions to gravitate ecclesiastically towards Constantinople. To check this process, Damasus had appointed the bishop of Thessalonica to be his Vicar throughout the Illyrian provinces. " They were included in the jurisdiction of the Pope, as Patriarch of the West."[2] Innocent, by *Cum Deus noster*[3] of 402, confirmed Anysius, bishop of Thessalonica 383-†410, in his Vicariate; and afterwards by *Lectissimo et*[4] of 17th June, 412, to Rufus, his successor 410-†31, he defined its extent and reminded him that it was from the favour only of the Apostolic See that his jurisdiction was derived. The Vicariate " manifested a certain vitality, and for nearly a century produced appreciable results." We shall meet it again under Pope Boniface—next

[1] H. H. Milman, *Latin Christianity*[4], i. 139.
[2] Duchesne, *Christian Worship*[5], 41.
[3] *Ep.* i. (*P.L.* xx. 463-5): Jaffé, No. 285.
[4] *Ep.* xiii. (*P.L.* xx. 515-7): Jaffé, No. 300.

successor but one to Innocent. But " the schism of long duration " between East and West " connected with Acacius, 484-519, " inflicted upon it a fatal blow."[1]

Passing to Gaul, we find Innocent consulted on various points of discipline by Victricius, bishop of Rouen 395-†415, and Exuperius, bishop of Toulouse 405-†15. Like other Popes, he knew how to make respectful language a basis for the exercise or the acquisition of an authority whether or not recognized by the applicant, and to turn every occasion to advantage. Victricius had visited Rome and was personally known to the Pope; and hence, perhaps, his request for information about the rules observed by the Roman church in various points of discipline. Innocent replied in *Etsi tibi, frater*,[2] of 15th Feb., 404, and sent him " this book of regulations to be carefully introduced to neighbouring peoples and bishops as a model," § 1; for he is anxious that " with the aid of the holy Apostle Peter, through whom both apostolate and episcopate in Christ took their beginning," the Church should be presented unto God " without spot or wrinkle," § 2. Victricius has done well in looking to the Roman church for a model; not that the rules he now sends, §§ 3-16, contain anything new; they are simply derived from the tradition of the Apostles and the Fathers, though too generally unknown or disregarded. Then follow the rules: and Innocent continues, § 5, by advising that " if any causes or disputes should arise, then let the quarrel be determined in

---

[1] Duchesne, *ut sup.*, 42.
[2] *Ep.* ii. (*P.L.* xx. 468-81): Mirbt[4], No. 145: Jaffé, No. 286

accordance with the Nicene Synod[1] by a gathering of
the bishops of the province, and let no one, saving the
rights of the Roman church to which in all causes
reverence should be observed, desert them in favour
of other provinces. If greater causes, § 6, are brought
into question, then, as the Synod (*sc.* Sardica taken
for Nicæa) requires, let them be referred to the Apostolic See. In this decretal Innocent is quite emphatic
about his authority in the West. He holds but does
not develop the Petrine theory. And he confines his
powers to the duty of seeing that the legislation of Nicæa
and of Sardica, which he takes for Nicene, is duly
observed. Next year, Innocent sent *Consulenti tibi*[2] of
20th Feb., 405, to Exuperius, bishop of Toulouse. He
had asked the advice of the Pope on several questions
of discipline; and received in reply a decretal in which
the Pope begins by commending his correspondent for
" following the habit of the wise, § 1, and referring
doubtful questions to the Apostolic See."

To the bishops of Spain Innocent addressed *Sæpe
me*[3] of 404 about the returning Priscillianists; but it
contains no reference, as is found elsewhere, to the
authority of the Apostolic See. He could afford to
assume that it would be taken for granted.

Coming nearer home from Spain to Italy, one of the
most important of the letters of Innocent, especially in
the liturgical field, is *Si instituta*[4] of 19th March, 416,

[1] Nic. c. 5.

[2] *Ep.* vi. (*P.L.* xx. 495-502): Jaffé, No. 293.

[3] *Ep.* iii. (*P.L.* xx. 485-93): Jaffé, No. 292.

[4] *Ep.* xxv. (*P.L.* xx. 551-61): Mirbt[4], No. 148: Jaffé,
No. 311: *Doc. Ch. Hist.* ii., No. 128.

addressed to Decentius, bishop of Eugubium—now
Gubbio—in Umbria. The see was situate in the
territory subject in secular affairs to the Vicar of Rome;
and was therefore one of the suburbicarian churches
whose bishops owed allegiance to the Pope as their
metropolitan. Customs proper to " the non-Roman
rite of the West," which prevailed over the border in
the territory ruled by the Vicar of Italy, had found their
way a few miles further south into Gubbio: and
Innocent was taken aback by foreign or non-Roman
rites so firmly rooted in a church of his metropolitanate.
He begins, § 1, by requiring uniformity in rites and
ceremonies, so that the faithful be not scandalized.
The Roman customs, § 2, " handed down to the Roman
church by the Prince of the Apostles, Peter, and here
kept until this very day, are to be observed everywhere:
the more so as throughout Italy, Gaul, Spain, Africa,
Sicily and the neighbouring islands, no churches were
founded save those for which the venerable Apostle
Peter, or his successors, provided bishops. Let them
enquire for any other Apostle in these regions. If
he cannot be found, then they ought to follow the
Roman church; for from it there is no doubt that they
had their beginning. Relying on foreign claims means
deserting the head." Innocent's assertions are bold
enough. He ignores the work of St. Paul in the West,
and makes large assumptions about the origins of the
churches of Lyons and the neighbourhood. On the
other hand, it is noteworthy that he claims an authority
for the Roman customs only in lands which, with Illyricum, make up the legitimate sphere of the Roman, or

Western patriarchate. And, no doubt, he is strictly
entitled in right, as in fact, to conclude by reminding
Decentius, § 16, that his church should in all things
observe the customs of the church of Rome, to which
it owes its origin. " Any further details you may
ask me, and I shall be able to tell you when we meet."

§ 3. Within a year, Innocent intervened in the
affairs of the church of Africa, at the request of its
episcopate. The Africans were concerned with Pelagianism; and sent three letters to him asking for his
support. The first[1] emanated from the Council of
Carthage, about midsummer, 416, begging him to
support them, § 2, " with the authority of the Apostolic
See." The second[2] proceeded, about the same time,
from the Council of Milevum, representing the bishops
of Numidia, who profess themselves convinced, § 5,
that the offenders would give way to the authority of
His Holiness, " drawn from the authority of the Holy
Scriptures." The third[3] was a private letter sent by
Augustine and four other bishops, pointing out that
the question is not whether Pelagius is or is not a
heretic, but whether the doctrine ascribed to him
should or should not find a place in the Catholic Church.
The three letters reached Pope Innocent early in 417;
and on 27th Jan. he answered in three several replies.

The first, *In requirendis*,[4] was addressed to the
Council of Carthage. The Pope begins, § 1, by con-
gratulating the Africans on having referred the matter

---

[1] Aug., *Ep*. clxxv.   [2] *Ib*., *Ep*. clxxvi.
[3] *Ib*., *Ep*. clxxvii.
[4] *Ep*. xxix (*P.L.* xx. 582-8): Mirbt[4], No. 149 (*a*): Jaffé,
No. 321.

—though they had done no such thing—to the " judgment " of his see, which he describes as " the source
of the whole episcopate "; and further on having so
acted " because the institutions of the fathers decreed
. . . that whatsoever was done in the provinces . . .
should not be taken as concluded until it had come to
the knowledge of this see." There is nothing in the
carefully-worded reference of the matter to Rome by
the Africans to suggest that they had acted on these
grounds, and no such " decree of the fathers " is known
to exist. All the more significant is it that this is the
passage on which Benedict XIV, 1740-†58, the most
learned of the Popes, relies in support of the opinion
that the *potestas jurisdictionis* is derived to bishops
not " immediate a Christo " but mediately through
the Pope. " The principle of monarchical[1] government, which Christ established in His Church, seems
to require that the source and origin of jurisdiction
over the whole Church should have its seat in that
visible head of the Church who is the Roman Pontiff,
and from him should flow forth into the other members.

[1] Note this question-begging assumption: and compare
Leo XIII on the relation of the Pope to the episcopate—
" Illud præterea animadvertendum, tum rerum ordinem
mutuasque necessitudines perturbari, si bini magistratus
in populo sint eodem gradu, neutro alteri obnoxio. Sed
Romani Pontificis potestas summa est universalis, planeque
sui juris; episcoporum vero certis circumscripta finibus,
nec plane sui juris: *Inconveniens est* [S. Thomas Aq.] *quod
duo æqualiter super eandem gregem plebem constituantur. Sed
quod duo, quorum unus alio principalior est, super eandem
plebem constituantur, non est inconveniens : et secundum hoc
super eandem plebem immediate sunt et sacerdos parochialis
et episcopus et papa.* See the *Satis cognitum* of 19th June,
1896, in E. Denny, *Papalism*, App. A, p. 716.

Hence Innocent:—' Knowing as we do what is due to the Apostolic See, since all who are placed here desire to follow the Apostle himself, from whom the episcopate itself and the whole authority of this name took its rise . . .' Clearer, and still more to our point, is Leo the Great:—' But this mysterious function the Lord wished to be, indeed, the concern of all the Apostles: but in such a way that He has placed the principal charge on the blessed Peter, chief of all the Apostles: and from him as from the Head wishes His gifts to flow to all the body.[1] " Benedict goes on to follow up this theory through St. Thomas, †1274, and St. Bonaventura, †1274, to Cardinal Bellarmine, †1621, who records it as one, though not the most probable, of the three opinions on the subject current in his day.[2] So Pope Benedict XIV.[3] But not so the Africans. They did not hold the monarchical theory of the Church and its powers as derived from Christ through St. Peter: a theory first put into shape by Innocent and finally rounded off by St. Leo.

The second, *Inter cæteras*,[4] of his three letters of 27th Jan., 417, contains his reply to the Council of Milevum. " You are aware," he writes, " that in all provinces, § 2, when questions are asked, replies (*responsa*) always proceed from the Apostolic source. Especially, as often as the reasons for faith are under

---

[1] Leo, *Ep.* x. § 1: see below, c. ix. § 1.
[2] Bellarmine, *Controversiæ*, Lib. IV (De Romano Pontifice), c. 22: Mirbt[4], No. 500.
[3] *De Synodo Diocesana* I. iv. § 2 (*Op.* xi. 7: Veneti, 1767).
[4] *Ep.* xxx. (*P.L.* xx. 589-93): Jaffé, No. 322.

discussion, then all our brethren and fellow-bishops, should in my opinion refer (*relatio*) to St. Peter, as to the author of their name and dignity, as you have now referred ": and then follows his opinion on the doctrinal point in question.

Finally, by *Fraternitatis vestræ*[1] he replied to St. Augustine and his fellow-bishops; referring to the letters of the two Councils as *relationes* and to his own replies as *rescripta*, § 1; and then, on the merits of the question, observing, § 5, that the book of Pelagius, which he had read, was enough to condemn him. " God have you in his keeping, dearest brethren."

These letters were almost the last to which the great Pope Innocent I set his hand; for he died 12th March, 417—" a prelate," says Milman, " apart from his rank and position," of " commanding character."[2] Their arrival in Africa caused the liveliest joy; and it was with reference to them, and to the rejoicings with which they were received that, in a sermon at Carthage of 23rd Sept., 417, Augustine expressed himself in a summary of the situation commonly but incorrectly quoted as *Roma locuta est : causa finita est*—as if the papal decision alone had settled the matter. But what he actually said was that " [Reports of] two Councils "—Carthage and Milevum—" have been sent to the Apostolic See. Rescripts have come from thence as well. The cause is finished."[3] It was finished on the joint authority of the two African

---

[1] *Ep.* xxxi. (*P.L.* xx. 593-7): Jaffé, No. 323.
[2] *Latin Christianity*[4], i. 112.
[3] Aug., *Sermo* cxxxi. § 10: Mirbt[4], No. 157.

Councils and the replies which the Pope had returned
to them. Elsewhere he says that " the matter was settled
by Councils, the Apostolic See, and the Roman Church
and Empire ":[1] and again he reminds the Pelagians
that " your cause has now been finished by a competent
decision of the bishops in common ":[2] *i.e.*, not by the
Roman see alone, but by the episcopate as a whole.

In Gaul and Spain the Popes dealt with distant
churches by decretals; and their letters were treated,
as in the official language of the day, as " rescripts "
in reply to " reports." The same terms were used
in correspondence with the Africans. But in Africa
the conciliar organization was as yet in full vigour: and,
in matters of discipline, so long as unity in doctrine
was secure, Africa claimed to be *sui juris*.[3] The Popes
were wise enough tacitly to admit the claim.

§ 4. Not very different was the relation between
Pope Innocent and the East, in the case of St. John
Chrysostom, archbishop of Constantinople 398-†407.
For a second time he had incurred the wrath of the
Empress Eudoxia; when, on Easter Even, 16th April,
404, as he was celebrating the rites of Baptism and
Confirmation in preparation for Easter Communion,
he and his flock were attacked and dispersed. He
sought the aid of Innocent in a letter preserved by his
biographer, Palladius.[4] The letter was not an appeal
in the later and technical sense; nor was it an appeal
to the Pope alone; for letters were sent in identical

[1] Aug., *De pecc. orig.* § 18: *Doc. Ch. Hist.* ii., No. 181.
[2] Aug., *Contra Jul. Pelag.* III. i. § 5.
[3] Batiffol, *Le Catholicisme de S. Augustin*, 441.
[4] *Vita*, § 2 (*Op.* xiii. 5-9: *P.G.* xlvii 8-12).

terms to Venerius, bishop of Milan, †408, and to
Chromatius, bishop of Aquileia, †407. It was a cry
for the aid of the West, as represented by three of its
leading prelates. He asks them to have no fellowship
with his rival Theophilus of Alexandria and his Synod
of the Oak, and to assure him of their communion:
protesting, at the same time, his readiness to defend
himself before an unbiassed tribunal. The letter was
brought to the Pope by four friendly bishops; but the
envoys of Theophilus had been there before them:
only the message which he had sent had been so curt
as to defeat its object.[1] Innocent accordingly wrote both
to Theophilus and to Chrysostom, saying that he
retained his ecclesiastical relations with each, but requiring an impartial Council to settle the dispute.[2]
It is interesting to note this proposal of the Pope.
The papal theory had already found formulation, and
some acceptance in the West. Innocent with the
Westerns habitually took a high tone and claimed to
exercise an appellate jurisdiction, as in his letter of
27th Jan., 1917, to the Council of Carthage; though in
Africa the claims of his see were not readily allowed.
But, in his support of Chrysostom, so far from regarding
himself as giving judgment, he endeavoured to get the
task undertaken by a Council: on the ground that,
according to the Nicene canons,[3] cases such as his should
be decided in the provinces where they arose. So he
wrote to Theophilus[4] and, again, to the clergy of Con-

---

[1] *Vita*, § 1 (*Op.* xiii. 4 D).   [2] *Ib.* § 3 (*Op.* xiii. 9 E, F).
[3] Nic. cc. 6 and 7.
[4] *Vita*, § 3 (*Op.* xiii. 10 C, D).

stantinople.[1] Innocent then had not, as yet, claimed for himself an authority equal to that of a General Council over the whole Church. Nor had Chrysostom assigned it to him. It is true that, in some places, Chrysostom uses very high language about the position of St. Peter. Referring, for example, in the *De Sacerdotio*, to " Feed my sheep," he argues that the reason why our Lord shed His blood was " to redeem the sheep whom he had entrusted to Peter and his successors."[2] But the context requires that " his successors " should mean not " all subsequent Popes " but " all succeeding bishops ":[3] and so does the general tenor of Chrysostom's teaching.[4] Once more, in this case, it is noteworthy how great was the difference between the papal attitude towards the East and the authority claimed by the Popes in the West; and St. Augustine is quite accurate in writing of Pope Innocent as " President of the Western Church ";[5] while Innocent himself was too discreet to claim more.

§ 5. Less discreet was his successor Zosimus, 417-†8, in the claims that he made over the Church in Africa: and he was forced to beat a retreat. For, if we may judge from his name, he was a Greek, and

---

[1] *Ex litteris caritatis vestræ : Ep.* vii. (*P.L.* xx. 501-7): Jaffé, No. 294, esp. § 3 (505 A) and § 4 (505 B): *cf.* Denny, *Papalism*, § 723.

[2] c. ii. § 1 : (*Op.* i. 372 B : *P.G.* xlviii. 632).

[3] *Ib.* § 2 : (*Op.* i. 372 D. : *P.G.* xlviii. 633).

[4] F. W. Puller, *Primitive Saints*[3], 124.

[5] [Occidentalis] ecclesiæ præsidentem — *Contra Jul. Pelag.* i. § 13 (*Op.* x. 503 F). Batiffol admits that the grammar seems to require " occidentalis," but holds that the argument demands " Romanæ." *Le Catholicisme de S. Augustin*, 484, n. 1.

can scarcely have enjoyed that long training in administration customary with the Roman clergy which produced from their ranks a succession of calm and wise rulers like Innocent I. Zosimus, says Mgr. Duchesne, was " a real anomaly,"[1] and his pontificate a series of blunders. First among them was the favour he showed to Patroclus, the intrusive bishop of Arles, 412-†26, on whom by *Placuit apostolicas*,[2] of 22nd March, 417, he not only conferred metropolitan authority in four of the provinces of southern Gaul to the detriment of existing rights, but made him papal Vicar over the whole of Gaul,[3] with powers like those of the bishop of Thessalonica in Illyricum. A second mistake was his patronage of Cælestius and Pelagius, who managed to enlist his sympathies.[4] Cælestius presented him with a confession of faith : and the Pope examined him before a local synod in the church of San Clemente. We do not possess its minutes; but we know what took place there from *Magnum pondus*,[5] the letter which Zosimus addressed to the Africans in Sept., 417. He assured them that " the faith of Cælestius was completely satisfactory ";[6] granted a delay of two months for further representations on their part; and suggested that, after all, the question at issue was curious and needless.[7] Pelagius also

---

[1] *Early History of the Church*, iii. 159.

[2] *Ep.* i. (*P.L.* xx. 642-5): Jaffé, No. 328.

[3] *Ib.* § 1 (*P.L.* xx. 643 A).

[4] Aug., *De pecc. orig.* ii. §§ 8, 9 (*Op.* x. 256: *P.L.* xliv. 388 sq.)

[5] *Ep.* ii. (*P.L.* xx. 649-54 and Aug., *Op.* x. app. 98-9): Jaffé, No. 329: Mirbt[4], No. 150 [a].

[6] " Absoluta Cælestii fides."   [7] *Ib.* § 6.

succeeded in securing the patronage of Zosimus, to
whom he sent various documents by the hand of his
friend Cælestius. On receipt of these, the Pope
summoned another synod: and, 21st Sept., 417, sent a
second letter—*Postquam a nobis*[1]—to the Africans, in
which he assures them of the *absoluta fides* of both
Pelagius and Cælestius taken together[2] and then of
Pelagius.[3] The letter arrived in Africa 2nd Nov., 417;
and Aurelius, the Primate of Carthage, at once took
action. Hastily summoning the few bishops at
Carthage, he suggested that Zosimus should leave
things *in statu quo* till he should be better informed
about the case; and then, when their numbers had
increased to two hundred and fourteen at the Council
of Carthage, Nov., 417, Aurelius and his colleagues
passed certain resolutions on the doctrinal aspects of
the question, and embodied them in a second letter to
Zosimus with the following preface: " We have ordained that the sentence which the venerable bishop
Innocent pronounced against Pelagius and Cælestius
shall stand "[4]—astonishing words to use to a Pope,
if papalism were true. But it saved respect for the
Roman see, and gently hinted to its then occupant
that, by contrast with his venerable predecessor, he
had been ill-advised. Zosimus had the good sense to

[1] *Ep.* iii. (*P.L.* xx. 654-61 and Aug., *Op.* x. app. 99-102):
Jaffé, No. 330: Mirbt[4], No. 150 [*b*].

[2] *Ib.* § 2.   [3] *Ib.* § 8.

[4] " Constituimus in P. atque C. per venerabilem episcopum
Innocentium de beatissimi apostoli Petri sede manere
sententiam." Prosper, *Contra Collatorem*, v. § 3 (Aug., *Op.*
x. app. 102 D, E: *P.L.* xlv. 1723 sq.): *Doc. Ch. Hist.* ii.,
No. 129.

take the hint, and began to retrace his steps. By *Quamvis patrum*[1] of 21st March, 418, he replied to the Africans in a letter remarkable alike for its grandiloquent language as to the authority of his See and for its practical surrender. " So great is our authority," § 1, he writes, " that no decision of ours can be subjected to review. It was for that very reason that we were anxious to carry you with us by consulting you at every step in regard to Cælestius; but, on reading what you have now sent us, § 2, we quite admit the need for deliberation, and we need only assure you that we have taken no final step, and that things are as they were in the days of Pope Innocent." The Africans saw to it that they should so remain. For they procured from the Emperor Honorius a rescript—*Ad conturbandam*[2] of 30th April, 418—banishing Pelagius and Cælestius, and then proceeded to deal with the letter of Zosimus at the Council of Carthage, 1st May, 418.[3] Blocked as he thus found himself both by Court and Council, Zosimus saw there was nothing for it but to proceed to the condemnation of Pelagianism. His sentence was embodied in a lengthy document, addressed to the bishops of the various countries, under the title of an *Epistola Tractoria*,[4] or Judicial Epistle, of which only fragments remain. The Church of Africa thus saved the Roman see from taking up with

---

[1] *Ep.* xx. 676-8 (Aug., *Op.* x. app. 104): Mirbt[4], No. 150 [c]: Jaffé, No. 342.

[2] Aug., *Op.* x. app. 105 sq.: *Doc. Ch. Hist.*, No. 133.

[3] Aug., *Op.* x. app. 106-8: Mirbt[4], No. 151: *Doc. Ch. Hist.* ii., No. 134.

[4] Aug., *Op.* x. app. 108 sq.

doctrinal error; and at the same time, made it clear
that by the Roman primacy they did not consider
themselves to be bound by orders from Rome.

§ 6. Zosimus was succeeded by Boniface I, 418-†22;
a priest of years and experience, a friend of Augustine,
who dedicated to him his *Contra duas epistolas Pelagian-
orum*,[1] and the trusted agent of Innocent I.[2] Boniface
was not less diligent than Innocent in asserting the
authority of his see; and his opportunity came in the
case of Perigenes, a native of Corinth, who was consecrated by its bishop, the metropolitan of Achaia, to
the see of Patræ. The people refused to receive him,
and he returned to Corinth. Soon afterwards, the
bishop of Corinth died, and the Corinthians demanded
Perigenes for their bishop, in a petition which they
sent to Boniface. The Pope was unwilling to take
action until he had consulted Rufus, bishop of Thessalonica, his Vicar in Illyricum; but, on receiving a
favourable reply, he confirmed the election, and Perigenes became bishop of Corinth. The bishops, however, who had opposed the election, and who also
disliked the papal interference in Illyricum, appealed
to the Emperor: and obtained from Theodosius II
a decree of 14th July, 421, in which, under plea of observing the ancient canons, he ordained that, if any
difficulty shall arise, in Illyricum, it shall be referred to
the assembly of bishops, not without the intervention
of the bishop of Constantinople: who, as bishop of

[1] See i. § 1 (Aug., *Op*. x. 411 A).
[2] Palladius, *Vita Chrysostomi*, § 4 (*Op*. xiii. 13 A: *P.G.*
xlvii. 15).

New Rome, had now begun to claim a prerogative equal to that of Old Rome.

Boniface, having received notice of this innovation and having also learnt that the bishop of Constantinople had summoned a Council to meet at Corinth and inquire into the consecration of Perigenes, wrote three letters, all of 11th March, 422, in which he enforces the primacy of his see by explaining on what authority he conceives it to rest.

The first is *Retro majoribus*,[1] addressed to Rufus. In it he reminds him that, as papal Vicar, he has behind him the authority of the blessed Apostle Peter; and so has nothing to fear from " those who make new claims and aspire to a dignity beyond their due," meaning the bishop of Constantinople: " for Peter does not suffer the privilege of his see to perish ": where Boniface assumes, as of course, not only that the Roman see is the see of Peter, but that Peter lives on in his see or, as we might say, that the see is Peter personified.

The second letter is *Institutio universalis*,[2] and is addressed to the bishops of Thessaly. Here the theory is further supported by the statement that " the foundation of the universal Church, at its birth, took its beginning from the office bestowed upon Peter, in whom its government and first-principle consists. For from him, as from its source, ecclesiastical discipline, with the growing observance of religion, has come to flow." Then follows an appeal to " the precepts of the Nicene Synod " in support of this

[1] *Ep*. xiii. (*P.L.* xx. 774-7): Mirbt⁴, No. 153: Jaffé, No. 363.
[2] *Ep*. xiv. (*P.L.* xx. 777-9): Mirbt⁴, No. 154: Jaffé, No. 364.

position, where the Pope appears to have in mind that preface to the sixth canon of the Council: *De primatu ecclesiæ Romanæ*, to the effect that " Ecclesia Romana semper habuit primatum ": which was quickly repudiated, when quoted as Nicene by the papal legate at Chalcedon:[1] and is thought to have originated in a version from Italy, unless it proceeded from Boniface himself ![2] A further appeal follows to the words of our Lord in the Gospel, very much as Damasus,[3] at an earlier stage of resistance to the rising pretensions of Constantinople, dismissed them with the reminder that his see had no need of conciliar support for its authority. It had the " voces evangelicæ," *i.e.*, the very words of our Lord in the Gospel, " Thou art Peter," etc., behind it. And, accordingly, Boniface continues: " Certain it is that, for the churches diffused throughout the world, this church is, as it were, a head over the members; and, if any one is separate from it, he is an alien to the Christian religion as having failed to remain in the body " thereof.

In the third letter, *Manet beatum*,[4] Boniface adds to the authority of the Nicene Council and of Scripture the appeal to precedent as in his favour. It was addressed to the bishops of Macedonia, Achaia, etc. —*i.e.*, to the members of the Council that was to assemble at Corinth to hear the cause of Perigenes, notwithstanding that it had already been decided by the Holy See. " What bishop after this," he writes,

[1] See below, c. ix. § 9.
[2] Batiffol, *Le siège apostolique*, 264 n. 1.
[3] See above, c. vi. § 6.
[4] *Ep.* xv. (*P.L.* xx. 779-84): Mirbt[4], No. 155: Jaffé, No. 365.

" could give orders for the meeting of such an assembly ?
If you read the canon, you will there find which is
the second after the church of Rome, and which is
the third; these great churches of Alexandria and
Antioch maintain their dignity by virtue of the canons,
with which they are well acquainted. They have
had recourse to the church of Rome in the matter
of more than common importance, as in the case of
Athanasius, and in that of Flavian of Antioch. For
which reason I forbid you to meet together to call
in question the ordination of Perigenes. But, if he
be accused of having committed any crime since he
was established in his see by our authority, our brother
Rufus, with such others as he shall choose to assist
him, will take cognizance of it, and report the whole
to us."[1] Boniface had already begun by saying that
the care of the Universal Church belongs to Peter by
the Lord's decree; and that such care, in matters of
importance, extends his responsibilities " even to
places in the East ": and he concludes by referring
all to Rufus, and threatening all who persist in taking
action apart from him with separation from communion
with the Holy See.

On one point Boniface is a little more accurate than
Damasus and Innocent: for they put Antioch, as the
earlier of Peter's two sees, before Alexandria, whereas
Boniface keeps to the civil and conciliar order of
Alexandria and Antioch; though he is at one with his
predecessors in regarding Rome and these two sees

[1] Fleury, *Eccl. Hist.* XXIV. xxxi. (tr. J. H. Newman, ii.
383 sq.).

as deriving their authority from a Petrine connexion. While thus mildly putting his predecessors straight, he also corrects Cyprian on a much more vital point. Cyprian's view of the episcopate turned upon the equality of bishops since " the other Apostles were what Peter was, endued with an equal fellowship of office and power."[1] Boniface insists that while " Bishops hold one and the same episcopal office,"[2] they should " recognize those to whom for the sake of ecclesiastical discipline they are bound to be in subjection."[3] We are thus within easy reach of that conception of the Roman Primacy to which Leo gave finality in his theory of the Petrine monarchy.[4]

§ 7. Cœlestine, 422-†32, succeeded Boniface without delay or contest. He was a Roman by birth; deacon to Innocent: a friend and correspondent of Augustine.

He maintained the authority of his see without difficulty in regions where it was already unquestioned. Thus to the bishops of Illyricum, by *Inter cæteras*[5] of 423-4, he asserted his right, as successor of St. Peter, to " a general oversight,"[6] and directed them to refer everything to Rufus, bishop of Thessalonica, his Vicar: and by *Cuperemus quidem*[7] of 26th July, 429, he dealt

[1] See above, c. iii. § 2: Mirbt[4], No. 66.

[2] " Sub uno eodemque sacerdotio ": *Ep.* xv. § 5.

[3] " Quibus propter ecclesiasticam disciplinam debeant esse subjecti ": *ibid.*

[4] Leo, *Ep.* xiv. §§ 1, 11: Mirbt[4], No. 171: and see below c. ix. § 1.

[5] *Ep.* iii. (*P.L.* l. 427-9): Jaffé, No. 366.

[6] " Necessitatem de omnibus tractandi."

[7] *Ep.* iv. (*P.L.* l. 430-6): Jaffé, No. 369: *Doc. Ch. Hist.* ii., No. 192.

en maître with the bishops of Vienne and Narbonne.
But, in other regions, less directly under his control,
and where the conciliar organization of the Church
was more developed, as in Africa and the East, he
had to be more discreet. He made a mistake indeed
in the choice of his legates—Faustinus at Carthage and
Philip at Ephesus—both of whom brandished the
claims of Rome rather too aggressively. But Cœlestine
managed to avoid a breach of communion, in spite
of them.

In Africa, soon after his accession, Cœlestine received
from Augustine a letter[1] about Antony, bishop of
Fussala, a small town about forty miles from Hippo,
§ 2. At Augustine's suggestion, though somewhat
hastily, he had been consecrated about 411-6, to that
see. He had misconducted himself in his office; had
been compelled by a synod of bishops to leave Fussala:
and had then applied to Pope Boniface for restoration.
Boniface had written in his favour, with the saving
clause, " if the information which he had given was
correct."[2] Augustine entreated Cœlestine to consider
the statement of facts which he now transmitted and
not to impose upon the people of Fussala, by the aid
of the secular power, a prelate so unworthy of the
dignity to which he had been inconsiderately raised.
He even went so far as to say that, as he was partly
responsible for Antony's appointment, he would have
to resign his see, unless the people of Fussala were
delivered from their bishop.[3] We do not know for

[1] *Ep.* ccix. [2] *Ib.* § 9.
[3] *Ib.* § 10.

certain what happened; but it is probable that Cœlestine wisely acquiesced.

§ 8. More serious in its effect upon papal relations with Africa was the case of Apiarius. He was no bishop like Antony: but, *c.* 417, a priest of Sicca Veneria, in Proconsular Africa. For serious offences he was deposed and excommunicated by his diocesan Urbanus, bishop of Sicca, a friend and pupil of Augustine.[1] He went off to Rome, and there sought redress from Pope Zosimus, with whom the first stage of the case of Apiarius began. Relations were strained at the moment between Rome and Africa: for Zosimus had just been forced to withdraw his protection from Pelagius and Cælestius by the pressure which Aurelius and his colleagues had exerted against him through the Court at Ravenna. Zosimus had an account to reckon with the African episcopate. So he took up the case of Apiarius: threatened Urbanus with deposition, if he did not retrace his steps: and sent Apiarius back with three legates into Africa— Faustinus, bishop of Potentia in Picenum, and Philip and Asellus, presbyters: the former of whom was afterwards sent by Pope Cœlestine to represent him at the Council of Ephesus, 431, in a similar capacity.[2]

Precedents were at hand, both " remote " and " recent,"[3] for appeals to Rome from bishops in Africa; but legates were an innovation. Zosimus may have borrowed the expedient from the practice of the Imperial Government: which, for instance, had sent

[1] Aug., *Ep.* ccxxix. § 1.   [2] See below, c. viii. § 3.
[3] Aug., *Ep.* ccix. § 8.

7

" the tribune and notary, Marcellinus,"[1] to preside
on its behalf over the Conference between Catholics
and Donatists held at Carthage in 411. While therefore Faustinus and his fellows were on their way,
Aurelius and his colleagues began to take action. At
the Council of Carthage, 1st May, 418, they forbade
appeals from " presbyters, deacons and inferior clergy "
on the ground that they had a remedy against their
bishop by " recourse to neighbouring bishops " and
thence to " African Councils or their Primates." But
the canon concluded: " ad transmarina autem qui
putaverit appellandum, a nullo intra Africam susci-
piatur."[2] This last clause seems to prohibit all appeals:
and that it was intended to do so is clear on the three
following grounds. First, a variant of the canon in
the collection of Dionysius Exiguus, †550, runs:
" They shall not appeal to a universal council, as has
often been determined about bishops: but whosoever,"
etc. Next Zosimus and finally an African Council in
writing to Cœlestine took it as prohibiting the appeal
of bishops to Rome, as will appear presently.

Thus much for appeals: but now for the legates. At
a small synod of Cæsarea Mauretania, 20th Sept., 418,
they were received by the Primate of Carthage and
invited to declare the nature of their commission.
They replied, at first, by word of mouth only: but,
pressed for their written instructions, they produced
them at last in the shape of a *commonitorium* in which
they were bidden to make four demands: (1) that

[1] Possidius, *Vita Aug.*, c. 13.
[2] Canon 17: Mirbt[4], No. 152.

bishops should have the right of appealing to Rome
—clearly Zosimus took the seventeenth canon of
Carthage as repudiating such right; (2) that bishops
should be forbidden too often to go to Court—he
was thinking, no doubt, of the African intrigues at
Ravenna that had recently caused him such humiliation;
(3) that priests and deacons should have a right of
appeal to neighbouring bishops—and who was nearer
neighbour to a bishop of Africa than the bishop of
Rome ? and (4) that Urbanus, bishop of Sicca, should
be excommunicated, or even sent to Rome, if he would
not cancel his proceedings in the case of Apiarius. As
to the second and fourth of these demands, they were
easily met. The African episcopate had already
legislated against going off to Court on frivolous
pretences; and Urbanus was perfectly ready to withdraw any decision of his that was reasonably open to
criticism. Moreover, the third requirement had long
ago been conceded; though what had it to do with the
case in question, unless the diocese of Sicca was ad-
jacent to the diocese of Rome ? But, along with the
first, it was pressed upon the attention of the Africans;
and, in support of these two demands, Zosimus
referred them to the fifth[1] and fourteenth[2] canon of
Sardica respectively: quoting these, however, in all
good faith,[3] not as Sardican but as Nicene. Naturally,
the Africans were unable to find them in the copy
of the Acts of Nicæa which had been brought back
with him by Cæcilian, bishop of Carthage, 311-†45.

[1] Hefele, *Councils*, ii. 120.
[2] *Ib*. 148.　　　　[3] *Ib*. 464 n. 1.

So they wrote to Zosimus and said that, pending investigation, they would observe " the two pretended canons of Nicæa," without prejudice. But the letter never reached him: for he died 27th Dec., 418; and was succeeded, at Easter, 419, by Boniface: who thus came to be concerned with the second stage of the case of Apiarius.

This was opened at the Council of Carthage,[1] 25th May, 419. Aurelius presided, along with Valentine, Primate of Numidia; next was seated Faustinus, the papal legate; then the bishops; then the other two legates who were only presbyters. On the motion of the president the copy of the Nicene Acts preserved at Carthage was read; then, on the demand of Faustinus, the *commonitorium* of Zosimus. But the reading of these instructions was interrupted by Alypius, bishop of Tagaste, as soon as the first of the two canons alleged to be Nicene had been recited. " I don't know how it is," he said, " but we did not find those words anywhere in our copies of the minutes of Nicæa "; and he moved that, as the original Acts were understood to be at Constantinople, Aurelius should write to the bishops of Constantinople, Alexandria and Antioch, and ask for authentic copies. Faustinus objected: let the Synod write to the Pope and ask him to institute the enquiry. But this would have been to place the decision in the hands of a party to the dispute; and, taking no notice of the opposition of the papal legate, the Council resolved that a copy of the Acts of Nicæa, as recited, together with the

[1] Hefele, *Councils*, ii. 465.

enactments of former African Councils (including therefore the seventeenth canon of the previous Council of
Carthage now in question) should be added to the
minutes of the Synod; and that Aurelius should write to
the bishops of Constantinople, Alexandria and Antioch,
to obtain from them copies of the genuine Acts of Nicæa.
If then the canons which Zosimus alleged were found in
these Acts, they were to be observed; but, if not, the
matter should be considered further in Synod. Meanwhile, they were to be observed provisionally: and,
of course, " what was decided at Nicæa has the
approval of the Council "—an important affirmation
on the part of the Africans: for hereby they made
quite clear the grounds on which they were making
the present concession, and at the same time reserved
their liberty of action for the future. As for Apiarius,
he made full confession of his offences; while Urbanus
his bishop corrected some informalities of the sentence
against him, and the offender was allowed to officiate
anywhere but at Sicca. A committee was appointed,
Augustine being one of the number, to draft a letter[1] to
Pope Boniface in pursuance of the resolutions. He was
requested to write for himself to the Eastern prelates
in whose churches " the truest copies " of the Nicene
canons would naturally be found; but, if on enquiry the
alleged canons should prove to be Nicene and to be observed as Nicene in Italy, " we will mention them no
more, and will make no difficulty about allowing them.
Such arrogance, however, as that of Faustinus, we do

---

[1] *Quoniam Deo placuit, Cod. can. eccl. Afr.* cxxxiv. (Mansi
iii. 831 B).

not expect to have to put up with again "; and they took care quietly to preclude any possibility of the word " neighbouring " by taking it for granted that it must refer to " the bishops of the provinces of Africa." We may observe, in passing, that, in this letter of Augustine and others on behalf of the African episcopate, there is no recognition on their part of any authority over them belonging to the Pope, save such as can be found in the legislation of Nicæa; while Zosimus himself, in seeking to base his action on Nicene enactments, offers testimony for his part equally incompatible with the later theory of papalism. He claims no directive but only an administrative authority. Even this claim turned out to be ill-founded. Of the deputation to Antioch we know nothing: but the replies from Atticus of Constantinople[1] and Cyril of Alexandria[2] are extant; and so is the Latin version known as " Attici," made at Constantinople for comparison with the " Vetus " or " Cæciliani " brought back to Carthage by that prelate. Needless to say the canons in question were conspicuous by their absence; and the Africans simply contented themselves by forwarding the documents to Boniface, 26th Nov., 419, as if the incident were closed.

It was reopened for its third and final stage under Cœlestine. Apiarius had taken up work at Tabraca, a city on the coast not far from Hippo. Here his conduct proved a repetition of the offences that had caused his removal from Sicca. He was excommuni-

---

[1] *Cod. can. eccl. Afr.* cxxxvi. (Mansi iii. 838).
[2] *Ib.* cxxxv. (Mansi iii. 835 sq.)

cated: appealed once again to Rome, and was received
by Cœlestine, who made the double mistake (1) of
restoring him to communion without hearing his
accusers and (2) of sending him back to Africa accom-
panied, as before, by Faustinus the legate whom the
Africans had found so overbearing. A Council at
Carthage was held to consider the situation. Faustinus
asserted " the privileges of the Roman Church," and
demanded that the decision of the Apostolic See
should be accepted as final. But the Africans did not
take this view of their liberties. They spent " three
days " in examining for themselves into the conduct
of Apiarius at Tabraca, Faustinus the while trying to
obstruct the enquiry and Apiarius to cover himself
by evasion. At last, however, the miserable creature
broke down, and confessed his enormities. The legate
was baffled; and the bishops, seizing their advantage,
wrote, c. 426, to Cœlestine an account of their proceedings in their Synodal Letter. It is the famous document
beginning *Optaremus*.[1] " We could wish that, like
as your Holiness intimated to us, in your letter sent by
our fellow-priest Leo, your pleasure at the arrival of
Apiarius, so we also could send you these writings
with pleasure, respecting his clearing of himself."
They then detail the enquiry to the point of the breakdown of Apiarius, § 1: and continue, § 2: " Premising
therefore our due regards to you, we earnestly implore
you that for the future you do not readily admit to
a hearing persons coming hence, nor choose to receive
to your communion those who have been excommuni-

[1] Cœlestine, *Ep*. ii. (*P.L.* l. 422-7).

cated by us, because your Reverence will readily per-
ceive that this has been prescribed by the Nicene
Council. For though this seems to be there forbidden
in respect of the inferior clergy or the laity, how much
more did the Council will this to be observed in the
case of bishops, lest those who had been suspended
from communion in their own province might seem
to be restored hastily or unfitly by your Holiness. Let
your Holiness, § 3, reject, as is worthy of you, that
unprincipled taking shelter with you of presbyters
likewise and inferior clergy, both because by no ordinance of the Fathers hath the Church of Africa been
deprived of this right, and the Nicene decrees have
most plainly committed not only the clergy of inferior
rank but the bishops themselves to their own metropolitans.[1] For they have ordained with great wisdom and
justice that all matters should be terminated where they
arise; and they did not think that the grace of the Holy
Spirit would be wanting to any province for the priests
of Christ [*i.e.* the bishops] wisely to discern and firmly
to maintain that which is right, especially since whosoever thinks himself wronged by any judgment may
appeal to the Council of his province, or even to a
general Council [*sc.* of all Africa]; unless it be imagined
that God can inspire a single individual with justice
and refuse it to an innumerable multitude of priests
[*i.e.* bishops] assembled in Council. And how shall
we be able to rely on a sentence passed beyond the
sea, since it will not be possible to send thither the
necessary witnesses, whether from weakness of sex or

[1] Nic. 5.

of advanced age or any other impediment. For that your Holiness, § 4, should send any [*sc.* legate] on your part, we can find ordained by no Council of the Fathers; because with regard to what you have sent us by our brother-bishop Faustinus, as being contained in the Nicene Council, we can find nothing of the kind in the more authentic copies of that Council. . . . For the rest, § 5, whosoever desires you to delegate any of your clergy to execute your orders do not comply, lest it should seem that we are introducing the pride of secular dominion [*sc.* the policy of sending representatives *a latere* borrowed by Zosimus from the Imperial Court] with the Church of Christ. . . . For now that, § 6, the miserable Apiarius has been removed out of the Church of Christ for his horrible crimes, we feel confident respecting our brother Faustinus that, through the uprightness and moderation of your Holiness, our brotherly charity not being violated, Africa will by no means any longer be forced to endure him. And so, Lord and Brother, may our Lord long preserve your Holiness to pray for us."

Thus Africa vindicated its right, in matters of ecclesiastical order, to remain *sui juris*,[1] while continuing in the unity of the Faith and without breach of communion. She recognized the primacy of the Roman See, so long as Rome made no claim to a primacy of jurisdiction. Cœlestine accepted the situation.

[1] Batiffol, *Le catholicisme de S. Augustin*, 441.

CHAPTER VIII

THE COUNCIL OF EPHESUS

§ 1. Not dissimilar were the relations of Pope Cœlestine with the East. Early in 429 he received copies of discourses by Nestorius; and wrote to Cyril of Alexandria asking for information. Cyril was in no hurry to reply. But, soon after Easter 430, he sent a *dossier* about Nestorius by the hand of his deacon Posidonius.[1] Thus in possession of information from both sides, Cœlestine summoned a Council in Rome, August, 430; and, in its name, replied to Cyril with *Tristitiæ nostræ*,[2] of 11th August. He commends, § 2, the zeal of Cyril in a cause which in truth is that of " Christ our God "; and desires him, § 4, " to join the authority of the Roman see to his own, and acting in our place," to let Nestorius know that, unless within ten days of the receipt of this admonition, he shall condemn his own doctrine by a written profession of the same faith as that which is held by the Roman, the Alexandrian and the whole Church, provision must be made for the see of Constantinople as if vacant, and Nestorius must be treated as one " separate from our body." Cœlestine, it will be noted, is not here professing to act as the sole and supreme judge or oracle of Christendom, or as the mouthpiece of the

[1] Cyril, *Ep.* xi.
[2] Cœlestine, *Ep.* xi. (*P.L.* l. 459-64): Jaffé, *Regesta*, No. 372.

Catholic Church. He announces his resolution, in concert with the Church of Alexandria, to break off all communion with the bishop of Constantinople, unless he retracts his heretical tenets. At the same time, he wrote to John of Antioch,[1] to the clergy and people of Constantinople,[2] and to Nestorius[3] telling him that he has appointed Cyril " to act on our behalf and to let our decision be known to you, and to all the brethren: for all ought to know what is being done, whenever a matter common to all is in hand."[4]

The messengers of Cyril reached Constantinople on 7th Dec.; but only to find that their business had been forestalled. For, on 19th Nov., the Emperor Theodosius II had summoned an Œcumenical Council to meet at Ephesus on 7th June, 431. Cœlestine acquiesced; and, along with instructions[5] sent on 8th May to his legates to the effect that they are to co-operate with Cyril and also to maintain the authority of the Apostolic See, he addressed *Spiritus sancti*[6] to the Council on the same day. It is a letter non-papal and conciliatory in tone; for, *more Romano*, Cœlestine is careful how he addresses Easterns. He concludes, § 5, by commending to them as his legates the bishops and Philip the presbyter—all of whom had represented him in the Apiarian affair. They are " to carry out what has been formerly determined by us " (*sc.* in

---

[1] *Optaremus quidem : Ep.* xii.: Jaffé, No. 373.
[2] *Ad eos qui faciunt : Ep.* xiv.: Jaffé, No. 375.
[3] *Aliquantis diebus : Ep.* xiii.: Jaffé, No. 374.
[4] *Ib.* § 11.
[5] *Cum Deo nostro: Ep.* xvii.: Jaffé, No. 378.
[6] *Spiritus sancti : Ep.* xviii.: Jaffé, No. 379.

the Roman Synod), " to which we doubt not that your Holinesses will give your assent."

§ 2. On 22nd June, the first session of the Council was held, with Cyril presiding.　His own see gave him the right to the chair: but the minutes record him as " holding also the place of the archbishop of the church of the Romans."[1]　This was not in virtue of Cœlestine's commission of the previous year,[2] by which he had been entrusted with the task of dealing with Nestorius, in the name of the Pope, unless within ten days he should recant.　Another process had supervened, viz. the Imperial project of a General Council.　Cyril's commission had lapsed.[3]　And, at the Council, though Cyril is recorded as having Cœlestine's proxy, just as Flavian of Philippi, for instance, signs three lines further down, as " holding also the place of " his superior " Rufus of Thessalonica," the Pope, on the arrival of the legates, was represented by them.　" Concurrently then ($\varkappa\alpha\iota$) with his own right of presidency," as Newman put it, " Cyril held the authority of the bishop of Rome."[4]　The Council then addressed themselves to the question of the Faith.　They read the Creed of Nicæa;[5] the second letter of Cyril to Nestorius,[6] which was declared by the bishops one by one to be consonant with the Creed and then approved by

[1] Labbé-Cossart, *Concilia* iii. 993 A.
[2] *Ep.* xi. § 4: as above.
[3] So L. Duchesne, *Early History of the Church*, iii. 243 n. 1; and W. Bright, *Age of the Fathers*, ii. 311.
[4] Fleury, *Eccl. Hist.* iii. 91 n. sq.
[5] Labbé-Cossart, iii. 1008 A, B.
[6] *Ib.* 1008 C.

acclamation; then *Aliquantis diebus*[1] of Cœlestine, and, finally, Cyril's *Cum Salvator*[2] of Nov., 430, to Nestorius which was received in silence[3] but without the anathematisms, about which Cyril now seems to have hesitated. At last, at the end of a long summer's day, the decision was taken and Cyril read the sentence of deposition and excommunication of Nestorius. Cyril signed first, but as bishop of Alexandria only; and the rest followed—each with the common formula —" una cum sancta synodo definiens subscripsi."[4]

§ 3. A fortnight or more followed before the arrival of the Roman legates in time for the second session on 10th July; when Cyril again presided as of his own right but " acting also as proxy for Cœlestine."[5] The legates were introduced: and, at their request, *Spiritus sancti*[6] of 8th May, 431, the letter of Cœlestine to the Council, was read. It was received with acclamations.[7] They place Cœlestine and Cyril on the same level; and hail " Cœlestine as of one mind with the Council."[8] The legates, indeed, ascribed more to the Pope than did the Council; and Philip, in thanking the Council for its acclamations, took them as an acknowledgment of the adhesion of the members to the head; whereas the Council had put it the other way round, acclaiming the head as of one mind with the members. " Holy members, by your holy voices, you

---

[1] *Ep.* xiii.
[2] *Ep.* xvii.
[3] Labbé-Cossart, iii. 1048 A.
[4] *Ib.* 1077 sqq.
[5] *Ib.* 1140 B.
[6] *Ep.* xviii.
[7] Labbé-Cossart, iii. 1148 A.
[8] *Ib.*

have joined yourselves to the holy Head: yea rather, by your holy exclamations. For your holinesses are well aware that, of the entire faith, or rather of the Apostles, the blessed Apostle Peter is the head,"[1] meaning Cœlestine. " A thoroughly Roman formula,"[2] as Mgr. Batiffol justly notes. But the Council took no notice.

At the third session, 11th July, the legates, having read the *Acta* of the first session submitted to them, gave their opinion that " everything had been decided canonically and in accordance with ecclesiastical order "; and concluded that " in accordance with the instructions of the most holy Pope Cœlestine . . . we desire to conform to your decisions."[3] The *Acta* of the first session were then recited. Whereupon Philip took occasion again to lay stress on the pre-eminence of the Roman See. " No one doubts, nay it has been well known in every age that the holy and most blessed Apostle Peter, chief and head and column of the faith and foundation of the Catholic Church, received the keys from our Lord Jesus Christ, the Saviour and Redeemer of the human race, and that authority to remit and retain sins was given to him, who to this very day and evermore lives on and exercises judgment in his successors."[4] Cyril, however, ignored this declaration: and asked the legates " as representing the Apostolic See and the bishops of the West "[5] to subscribe to the sentence against Nestorius. This

[1] Labbé-Cossart, iii. 1149 A.   [2] *Le siège apostolique*, 381.
[3] Labbé-Cossart, iii. 1151 D.   [4] *Ib*. 1154 E.
[5] *Ib*. 1158 D.

they did.   It is the more regrettable that the Vatican
Council quotes the words of Philip without any hint
that they emanated from the legate and not from the
Council.[1]   But this was not the view taken by the
Council of its own proceedings and the papal share
therein.   For, writing to the Emperor, they rejoice
that the legates had brought with them " the judgment
of the whole West, and had expressed sentiments
consonant with our own ";[2] while to Cœlestine they
report: " We also have decreed that the decisions taken
by your Holiness stand fast and firm."[3]

§ 4.   In the autumn of the same year, 25th Oct., 431,
a successor to Nestorius was found in the person of
Maximian well calculated to ensure the *entente* between
Constantinople and Rome: for Maximian was personally
known and appreciated there.[4]   A deputation was
sent to the Pope, with letters which informed him of the
condemnation of Nestorius and the election of Maximian.   We know of them only by Cœlestine's replies,
dated 15th March, 432.   In a letter[5] to the bishops who
had assisted at the Council of Ephesus, he regrets that
Nestorius had been allowed to retire to Antioch,
where he might make further trouble.   " You have
finished your business.   You have now to follow it up,
lest your labour be in vain.   The further away we are,
the closer our solicitude for the whole.   All are present

---

[1] *Constitutio dogmatica I de ecclesia Christi*, c. 1 (Mirbt[4],
No. 606, p. 462, ll. 28-34).

[2] Labbé-Cossart, iii. 1160 E.

[3] *Ib.* 1195 E and Cœlestine, *Ep.* xx. § 6.

[4] *Sixtus* III.: *Ep.* vi. § 7.

[5] *Tandem malorum : Ep.* xxii. (*P.L.* l. 537-44): Jaffé,
No. 385.

to the care of the blessed apostle Peter; and before God
we cannot refuse to take notice of what we know."[1]
In another letter,[2] to the clergy and people of Constantinople, he writes that " Blessed Peter the apostle
has not abandoned those in such serious trouble.
Everyone felt that the horrors of a gangrene like Nestorius had to be removed from the body of the Church,
and we have applied the knife and the dressing."[3]
Thus Rome, Constantinople and Alexandria were now
in communion, through the co-operation of the
Council with the Apostolic See. Such a primacy
of leadership and care for all the churches the
Council freely conceded to Rome. But they ignored
the claims put forward by the legate Philip, so
soon to receive final formulation in the theory of
St. Leo.

§ 5. Meanwhile, the next step was to reconcile the
see of Antioch: and this was the work of Sixtus III.,
432-†40: another Roman-born and another correspondent of St. Augustine.[4] Soon after his election Sixtus
sent a letter of 31st July, 432, to Cyril and his fellow-
bishops.[5] " We are only waiting," he wrote, " for
John of Antioch to come in. Let your colleagues
know. It is solicitude for all the churches which
forbids us to keep quiet in the face of anxieties like

---

[1] *Tandem malorum: Ep.* xxii. (*P.L.* l. 537-44): Jaffé,
No. 385 § 6.
[2] *Exsultatio matris : Ep.* xxv. (*P.L.* l. 549-58): Jaffé, No. 388.
[3] *Ib.* § 9.
[4] Aug., *Epp.* cxci., cxciv.
[5] *Gratiam habentes : Ep.* i. (*P.L.* l. 583-8): Jaffé, No.
389.

the present."[1] Happily the hopes of Pope Sixtus were fulfilled by the *Formula of Reunion*, April, 433, between Cyril and John. It was opposed by two metropolitans, Eutherius of Tyana and Helladius of Tarsus. They appealed to Rome, in terms which fully recognize the claims of Rome to intervene in the East.[2] But the appeal is to Peter *and* Paul: for they go on to adjure Sixtus to " imitate . . . Paul our fellow-citizen (*sc.* of Tarsus), and the companion of Peter, guardians alike of the nice balance of truth "[3]— so far are they from understanding the exclusively Petrine tradition as taken for granted in Rome itself. Then came the news of the reconciliation: and Sixtus addressed himself in two letters of 17th Sept., 433, to Cyril and John. In the letter[4] to Cyril he says that " the report (*relatio*) was as worthy of its sender as of the synod gathered to celebrate the anniversary of his consecration, to which he read it,[5] § 2. These congratulations of our fellow-bishops had for their witness the Apostle in whose person the episcopate began; for it was Peter himself who presided,[6] "§ 3. In the letter to John of Antioch[7] he bids him, § 5, rejoice that " the brethren have begun to dwell together in unity. You know now, by the issue of the present business, what it is to be of one mind with us. The blessed apostle Peter in his successors has handed on that which he received. Who would wish to separate

---

[1] *Ib.* § 6.   [2] *Ep.* iv. §§ 12, 13.
[3] *Ib.* § 14.
[4] *Magna sumus : Ep.* v. (*P.L.* l. 602-6): Jaffé, No. 391.
[5] *Ib.* § 2.   [6] *Ib.* § 3.
[7] *Si ecclesiastici : Ep.* vi. (*P.L.* l. 607-10): Jaffé, No. 392.

8

himself from the doctrine of him who was the first among the Apostles to be taught by the Master himself ?" § 5.

Three other letters of Sixtus remain to be considered; for they bear upon the papal Vicariate in Illyricum. In a letter[1] of 8th July, 435, addressed to the bishops of Illyria, he resists the attempt of the State, as evinced in the law of Theodosius II, 14th July, 421, which, however, was repealed at the instance of Boniface I, to detach Eastern Illyricum from the papal Vicariate. In a second letter,[2] of 18th Dec., 437, to the bishops of Illyria, he further resists its absorption by the Eastern Empire. All the churches of Illyricum, § 2, belong to the charge of the bishop of Thessalonica: questions are to be referred to him: councils are to be held by him: and the Apostolic See, on a report (*relatio*) made by him, is to confirm their proceedings. " So, brethren," § 3, " do not consider yourselves bound by those decisions of the Eastern Council which were made in opposition to our advice, but only by that part of them which concerns the faith and which had our consent." The reference may be[3] to the Council of Constantinople, 381; which by its third canon gave the second rank to the see of that city, to which the Popes never agreed. Or it may be[4] to a Synod of Constantinople recently held by Proclus, " that which concerns the faith " being probably " the Tome of

[1] *Si quantum : Ep.* viii. (*P.L. L.* 611-12): Jaffé, No. 394.
[2] *Doctor gentium : Ep.* x. (*P.L. L.* 616-18): Jaffé, No. 396.
[3] Fleury, *Eccl. Hist.* XXVI. xxxix.
[4] Batiffol, *Le siège apostolique*, 406 n. 3.

Proclus." The third letter,[1] also of 18th Dec., 437, was sent to Proclus himself. It exhorts him to maintain, § 1, " the ancient ordinances of the Fathers," *i.e.* in respect of Illyricum, and warns him to be on his guard against those who want to fish in troubled waters, *i.e.* bishops who resent the present régime there and would rather see Eastern Illyricum transferred ecclesiastically to the East. Let him therefore, § 2, receive none from thence, save those duly accredited. He then passes on to the case of Idduas, probably the bishop of Smyrna; who, under that name, appears as a signatory to the condemnation of Nestorius at the Council of Ephesus.[2] He had been accused before the bishop of Constantinople, and acquitted; but his accusers had then taken the case on appeal to Rome. It was a case like that of the two metropolitans who appealed against the *Formula of Reunion*; for " in the East, whenever Orientals find, or think they find, a miscarriage of justice, they turn to Rome."[3] This time, however, the Pope decided against them. He dismissed the appeal—*decrevimus judicium custodiri*, § 3— as if to show some deference to Constantinople.

Thus, as with his predecessors whose letters and doings we have now followed from Damasus onwards, " These various acts of Sixtus express the consciousness that he has of the care of all the churches incumbent upon him, the East included, as successor

---

[1] *Licet fraternitatem tuam : Ep.* ix. (*P.L.* L. 612-13): Jaffé, No. 395.
[2] Labbé-Cossart, iii. 1085 A.
[3] Batiffol, *Le siège apostolique*, 408.

of the Apostle Peter. It is clear that this primacy is an article on which the Easterns have to be humoured. They make much of it only when they want it. Sixtus, in his turn, only calls their attention to it with discretion."[1]

[1] Batiffol, *Le siège apostolique*, 409.

CHAPTER IX

ST. LEO THE GREAT

IT was for St. Leo—a Roman of the Romans—to establish the primacy of the Roman See and to provide it with a theory, or dogmatic basis, which has been held with little modification until embodied in the Vatican definition[1] of 1870.

§ 1. Leo's conception of the Roman primacy found expression first in the five sermons *De natali ipsius*[2] which were preached from time to time to an audience of bishops of his metropolitanate, some two hundred in number, assembled to celebrate the anniversary of his consecration.

Sermon I[3] was delivered soon after his " long journey " from Gaul, whither he had been sent by the Imperial Government to reconcile Aetius, the mainstay of Valentinian III and his mother Galla Placidia, with a smaller rival, Albinus. He had been elected in absence: and now thanks his flock for their " affectionate zeal " in electing him and asks for their prayers. It is a short sermon—as was his wont—and contains no allusion to the primacy.

But in Sermon II[4] he enters upon the topic of his right to rule. " The divine condescension, § 1, has

---

[1] *Const. dogm. de ecclesia I.* cc. 1, 2, 3 (Mirbt[4], No. 606, pp. 462-3).
[2] *Sermo* iv. § 4. [3] *P.L.* liv. 141-2.
[4] *Ib.* 142-4: *Doc. Ch. Hist.* ii., No. 225.

made this an honourable day for me. It has raised
my humility to the highest rank. The fostering condescension, § 2, and true love of the most blessed
apostle Peter is, I feel sure, not absent from this
congregation (sc. of bishops). He welcomes your
respect for the Lord's own institution, and commends
the well-ordered love of the whole Church which ever
finds Peter in Peter's see: and from affection for so
great a shepherd grows not lukewarm even over so
inferior a successor as myself. So entreat the good
God that He will render me, whom He has willed to
stand at the helm of the Church, sufficient for so great
a task."

In Sermon III,[1] the same doctrine finds further
expression. " Great is the condescension, § 1, of divine
grace which creates the bishop; and, § 2, great the aid
of the Apostles. For the solidity of that which was
praised in the Chief of the Apostles is perpetual; and,
as that remains which Peter believed in Christ, so
that remains which Christ instituted in Peter.[2] The
dispensation, therefore, § 3, abides; and the blessed
Peter, persevering in the strength of the rock which he
received, has not abandoned the helm of the Church
which he undertook. So, if anything is rightly done
and rightly decreed by us, it is of his work and merits
whose power lives and whose authority prevails in his
see. And so, § 4, we celebrated to-day's festival in
such wise that, in my humble person, he may be
recognized and he honoured in whom abides the care

---

[1] P.L. liv. 144-8: Doc. Ch. Hist. ii., No. 225.
[2] Matt. xvi. 16-19.

of all the shepherds, together with the charge of the sheep committed to them, and whose dignity is not abated even in so unworthy an heir as myself. And hence the presence of my venerable brethren and fellow-bishops, so much desired and valued by me, will be the more sacred and precious if they will transfer the chief honour of this service in which they have deigned to take part to him whom they know to be not only the patron of this see but also the primate of all bishops. Wherefore, when we utter our exhortations, believe that he is speaking whose representative we are."

In Sermon IV,[1] St. Leo develops another aspect of Peter's office. It is his to mediate the grace of Christ to his fellow-bishops. From the whole world, § 2, Peter alone is chosen: and, if Christ willed that there should be anything in common between him and other bishops, He never gave except through him that which He has not denied to others. Commenting on the keys of Matt. xvi. 19, he proceeds, § 3: " The rights of that authority passed over, indeed, to the other apostles as well, and the ordinance of this decree reached all the princes of the Church; but not in vain was that entrusted to one which was promised to all. To Peter was this unique grant made, that the person of Peter should be preferred to the rulers of all the churches. The privilege of Peter therefore still remains. . . ." Then, passing on to the exposition of Luke xxii. 31, 32, he continues: " In Peter therefore is the strength of all protected; and the aid of divine grace is so ordered that the firmness which is given by Christ to Peter

[1] *P.L.* liv. 148-52: Mirbt[4], No. 169.

should through Peter be bestowed upon the other apostles."

In Sermon V,[1] Leo dwells further on the relation between his own authority and that of other bishops. " It is true, § 2, that all the bishops taken singly preside each with his proper solicitude over his own flock, and know that they will have to give an account for the sheep committed to them. To us, however, is committed the common care of all; and no single bishop's administration is other than a part of our task."

The Epistles, of course, are occasional writings. All the more valuable then is the support which they give to the conception once for all set forth in the sermons.

Thus in a letter[2] of 445, addressed to the bishops of the province of Vienne about the case of St. Hilary of Arles, Leo writes of the preaching of the Gospel by the Apostles. " This sacred function, § 1, the Lord wished to be indeed the care of all the Apostles, but in such a way that He placed the principal charge on the blessed Peter, chief of all the Apostles; and from him, as from the head, wishes His gifts to flow to all the body; so that anyone who dares to secede from Peter's solid rock may understand that he has no part or lot in the divine mystery." In other words, the powers of the other Apostles were received not direct from Christ, but only through Peter. Apostles therefore are not Vicars of Christ, though they are so designated in the Proper Preface of the Roman Mass

[1] *P.L.* liv. 153-6.
[2] *Divinæ cultum* : *Ep.* x.: *P.L.* liv. 628-36: Jaffé, No. 407.

for the Feasts of Apostles—" Apostolos . . . quos operis tui vicarios contulisti præesse pastores ": the Pope alone has a right to that title.

This claim of the bishop to no more than a share of Peter's solicitude is further elaborated in another letter[1] of 445 to Anastasius, bishop of Thessalonica, whom Leo had made his Vicar in Illyricum:[2] " Seeing that, § 2, as my predecessors acted towards yours, so I too, following their example, have delegated my authority to you, beloved: so that you, imitating our gentleness, might assist us in the care which we owe primarily to all the churches by divine institution . . . we made you our deputy on the understanding that you were engaged to share our responsibility (in partem sollicitudinis), not to take plenary powers upon yourself (non in plenitudinem potestatis)." And again: " Bishops indeed, § 11, have a common dignity, but they have not uniform rank; inasmuch as, even among the blessed Apostles, notwithstanding the similarity of their honourable estate, there was a certain distinction of power; and, while the election of them all was equal, yet it was given to one (sc. Peter) to take the lead of the rest. From this model has arisen a distinction between bishops also, and by an important ordinance it has been provided that everyone should not claim everything for himself, but that there should be in each province one whose opinion should have the priority among the brethren; and again that certain

[1] *Quanta fraternitatis : Ep.* xiv.: *P.L.* liv. 666-77: Jaffé, No. 411, and Mirbt[4], No. 171.

[2] *Ep.* vi. § 2: *P.L.* liv. 617 B: Mirbt[4], No. 170.

whose appointment is in the greater cities should under-
take a fuller responsibility through whom the cure
of the universal Church should converge towards
Peter's one seat, and nothing anywhere should be
separate from its head."

Here we have a characteristic statement of Leo's
Petrine theory.   Once, however, when he was preaching
on 29th June, the Feast of St. Peter and St. Paul,
he lapsed into the older tradition: " Of these two Fathers
we must rightly make our boast in louder joy [than on
other Saints' Days]: for the grace of God has raised
them to so high a place among the members of the
Church that he has set them like the twin light of the
eyes in the body, whose head is Christ."[1]   In the same
sermon he recognizes the greatness of the city of Rome,
§ 1, and the extension of the Roman Empire as part of
the *præparatio evangelica*, § 2: but " through the blessed
Peter's holy see, thou [O Rome] didst attain a wider
sway by the worship of God than by earthly rule."[2]

Leo's conception of his office is thus clear and com-
prehensive. (1) He took the well-known Gospel
texts—the *voces evangelicæ* of Damasus—to mean that
supreme authority was bestowed by our Lord on St.
Peter. (2) He held St. Peter to have been the first
bishop of Rome, and (3) his authority to have been
perpetuated in his successors. (4) He conceived of it
as enhanced by a mystical presence of Peter in Peter's
see; and as having for its consequences (5) that the
authority of other bishops was not derived by them

---

[1] *Sermo* lxxxii. § 7 (*P.L.* liv. 427 A).
[2] *Doc. Ch. Hist.* ii., No. 227.

immediately from Christ but mediated to them through Peter, and (6) that, while their authority was limited each to his own diocese, his was a *plenitudo potestatis* over the whole Church, and the government of the Church rested with him.

We have now to consider how far these claims were admitted.

§ 2. In the West, they were freely admitted in Italy, where, for example, St. Peter Chrysologus, archbishop of Ravenna, 433 †54, in reply to a letter of Eutyches, 449, advises him to submit to the see of Peter, since " blessed Peter lives and presides in his own *cathedra*, and gives the true faith to all who seek for it."[1] In Spain, now separated from the Empire and under the sway of the Visigoths, the bishops turned towards the Apostolic See for the defence of their churches, because of the breakdown of synodical action among the local churches consequent upon the barbarian conquests. Turribius, bishop of Astorga in Gallæcia, confronted with the revival of Priscillianism, wrote for advice to the Pope. Leo replied with a letter[2] of 21st July, 447. He deals point by point with the errors of the Priscillianists: and concludes by saying that he has written to the bishops of the provinces of Tarragona, Cartagena, Lusitania and Gallæcia, enjoining a meeting of a General Council: and enclosing his " authoritative instructions for conveyance to the bishops of the provinces aforesaid."[3] Similar disorganization had taken place in Africa, upon the capture

[1] Leo, *Ep.* xxv. § 2.
[2] *Quam laudabiliter* : *Ep.* xv.: *P.L.* liv. 678-92: Jaffé, No. 412: *Doc. Ch. Hist.* ii., No. 228. [3] *Ib.* § 17 (692 A).

of Carthage by the Vandals in 439: but between 442 and 455 the western part of Numidia and the two Mauretanias reverted to Valentinian III. Leo had heard of irregularities there; and took advantage of the visit of an African bishop, Potentius, to Rome, to send him to make enquiries and to send in a report (*relatio*). On receiving it, he addressed a letter[1] of 10th Aug., 446, to the bishops of Mauretania Cæsariensis " impelled by that solicitude which by divine institution we bestow on the universal Church," § 1. He gives his decisions and directions in a manner as imperative as he would use to the bishops of his own metropolitanate: and it is a far cry from this letter of Pope Leo in 446 to *Optaremus* which the Council of Carthage had addressed to Pope Cœlestine twenty years earlier. The synodical organization of Africa had collapsed: the papal machinery of *relatio, rescriptum* and *legatus* had taken its place. " He seems in this to have substituted himself for the Council of Africa and the Bishop of Carthage, organs for the moment arrested. However, in a letter which gives evidence of his intervention, he does not in any way refer to their default: it is in virtue of the authority of the Apostolic See that he speaks and acts."[2]

§ 3. But in Gaul, two years earlier, Leo had had much greater difficulty in making his intervention effective; and only succeeded in doing so by calling in the State to his assistance. The case is that of St.

---

[1] *Cum de ordinationibus : Ep.* xii. (*P.L.* liv. 645-56): Jaffé, No. 410.

[2] Duchesne, *Early Hist. Ch.* iii. 435.

Hilary, archbishop of Arles 429-†49, and Celidonius bishop of Besançon in the province of Maxima Sequanorum, which had nothing to do with Arles. Celidonius, while a layman, had married a widow; and, as a magistrate, had given judgment in capital cases. Hilary, in company with his friend Germanus of Auxerre, 418-†48, visited Besançon, and for these irregularities assembled a Council and deposed him. " Hilary had without doubt acted in virtue of the right and even of the moral duty incumbent on every bishop to look about him and see that due regard should be paid to discipline ":[1] but, perhaps, owing to his monastic training, he may have been a little too austere. Celidonius, like others in Gaul before him,[2] sought redress at Rome; for Gaul, though outside the Roman patriarchate, was not outside the influence of the Apostolic See. If Hilary was inclined to exaggerate the authority of his see, Leo was not less bent on subjecting metropolitans to the Pope. Celidonius therefore received a cordial welcome.[3] Immediately, Hilary set off to cross the Alps on foot, though it was the depth of winter, and go to Rome. Arrived there, he entered his protest against the ease with which Celidonius had been received into communion by Leo, without examination of his case. He even affirmed that the Roman see had no right to review the decisions of Councils in Gaul: not even such rights as were conferred upon it by the Council of Sardica: for neither Leo nor the biographer of Hilary mention that Council, and apparently its

---

[1] Duchesne, *Fastes épiscopaux de l'ancienne Gaul*, i. 112 sq.
[2] Leo, *Ep.* x. § 2 (*P.L.* liv. 630 A).   [3] *Vita*, § 22.

legislation did not run in Gaul. Hilary's case was precisely that of the Africans, when they contended for the independence of their synodical judgments in the case of Apiarius. Not that he had come to make a formal appeal. He was there simply to let Leo know what he conceived to be the rights of the case. This done, Hilary, abrupt and austere as ever, returned, as he had come, unperturbed and afoot.

Leo, of course, was considerably annoyed. He, too, was an imperious person. He dismissed the charges against Celidonius,[1] and restored him to Besançon. Then he turned to Hilary, and treated him with an extreme severity. In a letter[2] addressed to the bishops of the province of Vienne, after an emphatic statement, § 1, of the prerogative of the Apostolic See, already quoted, Leo condemns, § 2, his arrogance; his rude language, § 3, such as " no layman could use and no priest listen to "; his encroachment, § 4, on provinces with which he had nothing to do; and, § 6, his recourse to the secular arm—so like that of Leo himself. Hilary therefore, § 7, was to cease to be metropolitan of Arles, and his rights were to be transferred to the bishop of Vienne. Let him " thank the clemency of the Apostolic See that he has been allowed to retain his bishopric !"

Leo meant not only to strike, but to strike hard. From the time of Damasus, his predecessors had known how to exploit the Imperial Government to their own advantage; and Leo procured, in support of his judg-

---

[1] *Ep.* x. § 3 (*P.L.* liv. 631 A).
[2] *Divinæ cultum : Ep.* x. *P.L.* liv. 628-36: Jaffé, No. 407.

ment, the celebrated Rescript of Valentinian III, dated 8th July, 445, beginning *Certum est.*[1] After reciting " the primacy of the Apostolic See " and the behaviour, § 1, of Hilary from the papal point of view, and noting, § 2, the sentence pronounced against him, the Emperor proceeds: " We decree, § 3, by this perpetual edict that it shall not be lawful for the bishops of Gaul or of the other provinces, contrary to ancient custom, to do aught without the authority of the Venerable Pope of the Eternal City; and whatsoever the authority of the Apostolic See has enacted, or may hereafter enact, shall be the law for all. So that, if any bishop summoned to trial before the Pope of Rome shall neglect to attend, he shall be compelled to appear by the governor of the province; in all respects, regard being had to the privileges which our deified parents (*sc.* Gratian) conferred on the Roman church. Wherefore Your Illustrious and Eminent Magnificence (*sc.* Aetius) is to cause what is enacted above to be observed in virtue of this present edict and law, and a fine of ten pounds is at once to be levied on any judge who suffers our Commands to be disobeyed." The result of this enactment was to go far beyond the grant of Gratian[2] to which it refers: and to rivet a papal autocracy on the Western Empire—or what remained of it—by the whole force of the civil law. Not only was Leo's condemnation of Hilary brought officially, by this Rescript, to the cognizance of the Patrician

[1] Leo, *Ep.* xi.: *P.L.* liv. 636-40: Mirbt[4], No. 172: *Doc. Ch. Hist.* ii., No. 206.
[2] *Ordinariorum sententiæ* (*P.L.* xiii. 583-8); and above, c. vi. § 2.

Aetius; but, should any bishop, in Gaul or elsewhere, be cited by the Pope to appear before him, he must at once obey the summons or, in case of refusal, be constrained by the secular arm to present himself at Rome. It is the crowning proof that the papacy at Rome—as distinct from the primacy of the Apostolic See in Christendom—is the creation of the State. " There is nothing more absolutely certain in the history of the Church than that the papal jurisdiction, outside the suburbicarian provinces, mainly arose out of the legislation of the State. Erastianism begat it; and forgery[1] developed it."[2]

Hilary, for a time, took no further notice; but confined himself to the charge of his diocese. Later he sent envoys to appease the wrath of Leo;[3] and Auxiliaris, a mutual friend of his and Leo's, now living in retirement at Rome, after having served as Prætorian Prefect of Gaul, endeavoured to make peace for him; at the same time bidding Hilary reflect that " Roman ears are sensitive, but open to deferential language; if your Holiness would but unbend a little in that way, you would lose little and gain much."[4] But Hilary remained until his death, 5th May, 449, as unmoved as Leo: and he is now a Saint of the Roman Martyrology,[5] though he may have died out of communion with the

---

[1] *E.g.*, The Forged Decretals, *c.* 845 (Mirbt[4], No. 252), and the *Thesaurus Græcorum Patrum*, which deceived St. Thomas Aquinas,†1274 (*ib.*, No. 361).

[2] F. W. Puller, *The Primitive Saints and the See of Rome*[3], 196.

[3] *Vita*, § 22.   [4] *Ibid.*

[5] *Acta SS. Maii*, ii. 24: Præf. § 3.

see of Rome.[1] The situation improved with his successor Ravennius, 449-†55; for Leo, at that time, was seeking the assent of the West to his Tome.[2] He could not afford to forgo the unanimous backing of the church of Gaul; and in a letter[3] of 5th May, 450, addressed to the comprovincials of Arles, who had written to him to announce the consecration of Ravennius and to protest against the claims of Vienne[4] to primacy, he settled the rivalry between Arles and Vienne. In return, Milan,[5] Gaul[6] and Spain[7] gave in their adherence to the Tome; and the Pope, on 27th Jan., 452, was in a position to inform Ravennius[8] that all had gone well with his intervention at the Council of Chalcedon.

The relation of Leo to the Council of Chalcedon, 451, must occupy our attention next.

§ 4. The events leading to Chalcedon were consequent upon a reaction against the decisions of Ephesus, 431. In spite of the reconciliation effected between Cyril and John by the *Formula of Reunion*, 433, the ultra-Cyrilline party was waiting its opportunity. They clung to Cyril's formula—" one incarnate nature (φύσις) of God the Word "; and, whereas by nature (φύσις) Cyril meant the same as others meant by person

---

[1] So Tillemont xv. 80, 89: and Fleury xxvii. c. 5: but there is a doubt: see F. W. Puller, *Primitive Saints and the See of Rome*[3], 199 n. 2.

[2] *Ep.* xxviii. (*P.L.* liv. 755-82).

[3] *Lectis dilectionis vestræ : Ep.* lxvi. (*P.L.* liv. 883-6).

[4] *Ep.* lxv. § 2 (*P.L.* liv. 880 sq.).

[5] *Ep.* xcvii.   [6] *Ep.* xcix.   [7] *Ep.* cii. § 5.

[8] *Optassemus quidem : Ep.* cii. (*P.L.* liv. 983-6): Jaffé, No. 479.

(ὑπόστασις),[1] they took the word in its ordinary meaning, and so were known as Monophysites. Of these, the chief exponent in Constantinople was the abbot Eutyches. His godson was Chrysaphius, the eunuch all-powerful with Theodosius II. When therefore Eutyches came into conflict with Flavian, archbishop of Constantinople, he could count on the support of the Emperor. He could also count on Dioscorus, recently elected archbishop of Alexandria, 444-51; for not only was Dioscorus leader of the ultra-Cyrillines, but he would not be likely to miss an opportunity of humiliating the see of Constantinople, as his predecessors Theophilus and Cyril had made the most of such opportunities in their day. At first, he did not show his hand: but announced his accession to Leo in the accustomed form of an Enthronistic Letter. Leo replied[2] as courteously in a letter of 21st June, 445: but took occasion to remind him, § 1, of the relation between the see of St. Mark and the see of St. Peter. " You and we ought to be at one: for since the most blessed Peter received the primacy (principatus) of the Apostles from the Lord, and the church of Rome still abides by his institutions, it is wrong to believe that his holy disciple Mark, who was the first to govern the church of Alexandria, formed his decrees on a different line of tradition." Relations between Leo and Eutyches were at first equally correct; and Eutyches, anxious to secure the goodwill of Rome, wrote in May,

[1] For Cyril's explanations of his meaning, see my *Hist. Ch. to A.D.* 461, iii. 266 and the references there.

[2] *Quantum dilectioni tuæ : Ep.* ix. (*P.L.* liv. 624-7): Jaffé, No. 406.

448 to inform him that Nestorians were on the increase.
But these " Nestorians " were, in fact, Catholics; and
Leo cautiously replied,[1] 1st June, 448, commending
his zeal and saying that he would make further enquiries.
Then the situation changed; and Eutyches found himself no longer plaintiff but defendant; for on a charge of
heresy made against him by Eusebius, bishop of Dorylæum, at the synod of Constantinople, 8th-22nd Nov.,
448, he was condemned for his opinions by archbishop
Flavian.   He would appeal, he retorted, to the Councils
of Rome, Alexandria, Jerusalem and Thessalonica;
thus coupling Rome with other sees, and omitting
Antioch because it was on the other side.   But he
counted most on Rome.   He wrote at once to Leo,[2]
Nov., 448: " I take refuge," he said, " with you, the
defender of religion; conscious that I have never
innovated on the Faith."   Chrysaphius took care that
the case of his godfather should be seconded by a
letter from Theodosius himself;[3] while Eutyches took
the precaution of soliciting the aid of St. Peter Chrysologus, archbishop of Ravenna, the capital of Valentinian III and the Western Court.   The archbishop,
early in 449, advised him obediently to await the letters
of Leo, in terms that we have already quoted.[4]   The
Petrine theory, as put into final shape by Leo, was
thus clearly accepted by distinguished prelates of the
West.   Leo was not long in taking action.   On

[1] *Ad notitiam nostram* : *Ep.* xx. (*P.L.* liv. 713-14): Jaffé,
No. 419.
[2] Leo, *Ep.* xxi. (*P.L.* liv. 713-18).
[3] Leo, *Ep.* xxiv § 1.
[4] See above, c. ix. § 2.

18th Feb. he wrote to Flavian[1] and to the Emperor,[2] asking for further information. No sooner were these letters sent off than it reached him in Flavian's first letter to Leo.[3] He sends the minutes of the Synod of Constantinople, that the Pope may make the case known to " all the bishops in office under your Reverence ": but makes no reference to any further prerogative. Rome, in his eyes, was still the centre of communications between East and West, rather than of communion. On 21st May, Leo acknowledged[4] the letter, and foreshadowed the Tome. It was already in preparation; and was dispatched[5] to Flavian, 13th June, 449, as containing the Pope's mature judgment. Scarcely had the post gone when a second letter[6] arrived from Flavian. He deprecated a Council: " the matter only requires your weight and support."[7] The request to declare a Council unnecessary went home to willing ears: and, 20th June, Leo replied[8] " that in his view too there was no need of a synod to deal further with the matter." But it was too late. Neither Flavian nor Leo could prevent it. For

---

[1] *Cum Christianissimus* : *Ep.* xxiii. (*P.L.* liv. 731 sqq.): Jaffé, No. 420.

[2] *Quantum præsidii* : *Ep.* xxiv. (*P.L.* liv. 734-6): Jaffé, No. 421.

[3] Leo, *Ep.* xxii. (*P.L.* liv. 723-8).

[4] *Pervenisse ad nos* : *Ep.* xxvii. (*P.L.* liv. 751-2): Jaffé, No. 422.

[5] *Lectis dilectionis tuæ:* *Ep.* xxviii. (*P.L.* liv. 755-82): Jaffé, No. 423.

[6] Leo, *Ep.* xxvi. (*P.L.* liv. 743-52).

[7] *Ib.* 747 B.

[8] *Lectis dilectionis tuæ* : *Ep.* xxxvi. (*P.L.* liv. 809-11): Jaffé, No. 430.

Eutyches had made interest at Court again; and by *Cunctis constitit*[1] of 30th March addressed to Dioscorus and others, Theodosius had summoned a Council to meet at Ephesus in Aug., 449. It has come down to history, by the name which Leo gave it,[2] as the *Latrocinium* or Robber-Council of Ephesus.

Leo received the letter of summons on 13th May,[3] and appointed as his legates Julius, bishop of Puteoli; Renatus, a presbyter who died on the way, and Hilary, a deacon, who afterwards succeeded him as Pope. They left Rome before midsummer: and carried with them a batch of letters,[4] dated 13th June—(1) the Tome, addressed to Flavian, (2) to Theodosius, (3) to Pulcheria, (4) to the archimandrites of Constantinople, (5) to the Synod, with (6) and (7) to his agent, Julian, bishop of Cos. As Julian spoke both Greek and Latin, and the legates Latin only, it was important that he should be well briefed in their support. Leo explained to Pulcheria why he could not come himself: there was no precedent, and he might, at any moment, have to deal with Attila, King of the Huns.[5] To the Synod he commends " the devout faith of our Most Clement Prince who has paid such deference to the divine institutions [*sc*. Matt. xvi. 13-18] as to apply to the authority of the Apostolic See for a proper settlement."[6] The Synod, however, from 8th-22nd Aug., paid little attention to Peter or Leo. It was dominated by Dios-

---

[1] Mansi vi. 587-90.   [2] *Ep*. xcv. § 2.   [3] *Ep*. xxxi. § 4.
[4] *P.L.* liv. 755-810: Jaffé, Nos. 423-9.
[5] *Ep*. xxxi. § 4.   [6] *Ep*. xxxiii. § 1.

corus, as president, with armed force at his disposal. He set aside the papal letters, which the legates desired to have read, and proceeded at once to reinstate Eutyches and to depose Flavian. " I disdain your authority," cried Flavian. *Contradicitur*,[1] exclaimed the legate Hilary. He made good his escape to Rome: and in the baptistery of the Lateran may still be seen the inscription which he put up when Pope, 461-†8, in remembrance of his escape, to the honour of " his liberator, St. John the Evangelist."[2]

Hilary was thus able to bring a first-hand report to Leo of all that had taken place at the *Latrocinium*; and the Pope immediately put himself at the head of the reaction, 449-50, which set in against it.

§ 5. He received three appeals.

The first was the *Libellus appellationis*[3] of Flavian, which Hilary had brought with him. It was addressed to " archbishop Leo ": and Flavian recalls " the appeal " which he had made in the midst of the tumult at Ephesus " to the throne of the Apostolic See of St. Peter, the Prince of the Apostles, and to the holy Council in general (*i.e.* to the usual synod of bishops in Rome) which meets under your Holiness."[4] He then requests the Pope to " issue a decree that a united synod of the Fathers both of East and West may be held . . . and all be brought to nothing and undone which has now been effected by a sort of gamester's

[1] Mansi vi. 908 D.

[2] Duchesne, *Early History of the Church*, iii. 292 n. 1.

[3] *Church Historical Society's Pamphlets*, No. lxx., ed. T. A. Lacey (S.P.C.K.), and Mirbt[4], No. 173.

[4] *Ib.*, p. 50, ll. 162-6.

trick."[1] Flavian recognizes the primacy of the
Apostolic See. But it is a primacy of leadership, not
of jurisdiction.

A second appeal came from Eusebius, bishop of
Dorylæum, who with Flavian had been deposed at
Ephesus.[2] In his *Libellus appellationis*[3] he begs Leo
to take action in support of his legates there who had
demanded in vain from Dioscorus that he, as well as
Eutyches, the one the plaintiff, the other the defendant
at the Synod of 448, should be heard;[4] and he " begs
to be restored to the episcopal dignity and your
communion."[5] No mention is made of Leo's episcopal
synod. Eusebius has merely " presented a libel of
appeal demanding audience of your see."[6] " We can
scarcely be surprised," says Canon Lacey, " that
Flavian in his desperate cry for help, and Eusebius in
his more matured plea, were alike disposed to exalt
the authority of the Roman See. It was their only
refuge."[7] But probably they would have agreed with
Theodoret as to the grounds on which this authority
rested.

The appeal of Theodoret,[8] bishop of Cyrrhus, is
the third of those addressed to Leo at this junc-
ture. He begins, § 1, by acknowledging the primacy
(τὸ πρωτεύειν) of the Roman See, and its many privileges
(πλεονεκτήμασι). " Rome is of all cities the greatest

[1] *C.H.S.*, p. 52, ll, 208-18.   [2] Mansi vi. 908 B, C.
[3] *C.H.S.*, No. lxx. 53-8: Mirbt[4], No. 174.
[4] *C.H.S.*, No. lxx. 56.   [5] *Ib*. 58, ll. 413-15.
[6] *Ib*., ll. 400-4.   [7] *Ib*. 33.
[8] Leo, *Ep*. lii. (*P.L.* liv. 845-51): *Doc. Ch. Hist*. ii., No.
224.

and most famous, the mistress of the world and teeming with population. . . . She has also the tombs of our common fathers and teachers of the truth, Peter and Paul. They have rendered your see so glorious; and their see (not the see of Peter only) is still blest by the light of their God's presence, seeing that therein He has placed your Holiness to shed abroad the rays of the one true faith." Candid but unwelcome felicitations; for " Leo would never have assigned the see of Rome to St. Paul,"[1] and Innocent X, 1644-†55, condemned as heretical certain phrases of Antoine Arnauld in *De la fréquente communion* which involved " an equality between St. Peter and St. Paul, without any subordination and subjection of St. Paul to St. Peter in the supreme power and government of the universal Church."[2] But Theodoret was merely repeating the older tradition of Rome itself, as preserved in the inscriptions of the Catacombs, in the Roman episcopal lists, and in the Latin Mass— a tradition displaced early in the third century by the belief that Peter alone was the Apostolic founder and first bishop. Theodoret then goes on, § 2, to thank the Pope for his Tome to Flavian; and, § 3, to complain of the injustice of Dioscorus, who had condemned him in absence. " My life, § 4, and my writings, § 5, testify to the soundness of my faith. Do not therefore spurn my petition (ἱκετίαν) ": for such it was, not a judicial appeal. This letter to the Pope was supported by others[3] in the same strain to his *entourage*: among

---

[1] Batiffol, *Le siège apostolique*, 518 n. 2.
[2] Mirbt[4], No. 528.   [3] *Epp.* cxvi.-cxix.

them, one to Renatus, of whose death Theodoret was still unaware, in which he acknowledges " the hegemony of the holy throne of Rome over the churches of the world ": not, indeed, on the ground that the office of Supreme Pastor belongs *jure divino* to the Roman bishop (as if, with Athens of old, the hegemony had become a monarchy[1]), but on account of its faith, which was " never," he says, " sullied by heresy."[2]

§ 6. A Council in Rome was celebrating the anniversary, 29th Sept., 449, of Leo's consecration when these appeals arrived. They discussed the situation: and, in their name and his own, the Pope dispatched seven letters[3] in all, 13th-15th Oct., to protest against the proceedings of Ephesus. The first of these[4] was addressed to the Emperor Theodosius II. He requests, § 3, that all may remain *in statu quo*, until its doings are revised by " a General Council to be held in Italy . . . to which the bishops of the Eastern provinces must come; and how necessary this request is after the lodging of an appeal (*sc.* by Flavian) is witnessed by the canonical decrees passed at Nicæa, which are added below." But the canon is Sardican: and Leo can hardly have been unaware of it.[5] There was no reply: and, getting impatient, on Christmas Day, 449, he sent off a second letter[6] to Theodosius, asking whether he had received his former communication. Still no reply: when,

---

[1] Thucydides i. 75 and 96, 97.
[2] *Ep.* cxvi. (*P.G.* lxxxiii. 1325).
[3] *Epp.* xliv., xlv., xlvii.-li.: Jaffé, No. 438-44.
[4] *Ep.* xliv. (*P.L.* liv. 827-32).
[5] C. Gore, *Leo the Great*, 113-14.
[6] *Pro integritate fidei* (*P.L.* liv. 855-6): Jaffé, No. 445.

21st Feb., 450, the Western Court came to Rome and took part, next day, in the Feast of St. Peter's Chair. Leo contrived to turn the occasion to account. At his suggestion Valentinian III, his mother Galla Placidia, and his wife Eudoxia, each wrote[1] to their Eastern kinsfolk. Valentinian, prompted, no doubt, by Leo as in his decree directed against Hilary of Arles, makes much[2] of the respect due to St. Peter and of the right of the bishop of Rome, " on whom ancient usage has conferred a pre-eminence in the episcopate above all others to judge in matters of faith and [in the case of] bishops." The allusion again is to the Sardican canon. His mother, Galla Placidia, writes[3] in similar terms; making the same claim for the Apostolic See, " in accordance with the provisions of the Nicene [*i.e.* Sardican] canon."[4] But nothing came of these representations. Theodosius had but just issued a rescript confirming everything that was done at Ephesus. He sent frigid replies to the Pope (not extant); and to the Emperor and Princesses of Ravenna.[5] " Peace and concord," he assured Valentinian, " reign in the churches of our dominions," as much as to say, " We can look after ourselves, and the East does not want any supervision by the West." The letter may well have been dictated by Chrysaphius: but it was almost the last that Theodosius wrote, for on 28th July, 450, he was thrown from his horse and killed. At once,

---

[1] Leo, *Epp.* lv.-lviii. (*P.L.* liv. 857-72).
[2] *Cum advenissem : Ep.* lv. (*P.L.* liv. 857-60).
[3] *Dum in ipso : Ep.* lvi. (*P.L.* liv. 859-62).
[4] *Ib.* 861 B.
[5] *Epp.* lxii.-lxiv. (*P.L.* liv. 875-80).

the whole situation, political and ecclesiastical, was reversed: and the way was open for Leo, in concert with Pulcheria and Marcian, the new Sovereigns of the East, and in co-operation with the Council of Chalcedon, to restore the Faith.

It was, perhaps, because Leo knew that he could count on the Eastern Court that his zeal to redress the wrongs of Ephesus by another Council began to cool. He would also reflect that, if there was to be a Council, as the two Emperors Valentinian III and Marcian now desired in a letter[1] which they addressed to him, Aug.-Sept., 450, the prospect of holding it, as he had proposed, in Italy, where he could control it, would be fainter under Marcian and Pulcheria, who knew their own mind,[2] than under the weak rule of Valentinian III. Accordingly, when he had received Marcian's summons of 17th May, 451, to a Council in the autumn, Leo, though he had thought the time inopportune, politely acquiesced. " I make no objection," he wrote in § 1 of a letter[3] of 26th June, and added that he would himself be present, § 2, in the legates whom he had already appointed[4] on 24th June. They were Paschasinus, bishop of Lilybæum in Sicily, and Boniface, a presbyter, with whom he also associated his envoys already in the East. He provided them each with a copy of the Tome, and with further instructions,[5] while Boniface, who set off direct from Rome, carried

---

[1] *Ad hoc maximum*: Leo, *Ep.* lxxiii. (*P.L.* liv. 899-900).
[2] *Epp.* lxxvi., lxxvii., of 22nd Nov., 450 (*P.L.* liv. 903-8).
[3] *Poposceram : Ep.* xc. § 1 (*P.L.* liv. 932-4): Jaffé, No. 470.
[4] *Ep.* lxxxix. (*P.L.* liv. 930 sq.): Jaffé, No. 469
[5] *Ep.* lxxxviii. (*P.L.* liv. 927-9).

letters of 26th June[1] to the Emperor, to Anatolius, bishop of Constantinople, to Julian of Cos, and to the Council. In the last of these,[2] to the Council, he says, § 1, that he will preside in his legates. There is no need, § 2, to discuss the Faith; it had already been sufficiently set forth in his Tome to Flavian. The only question is, § 3, to restore the ejected bishops and to maintain the decisions of Cyril and the Council of Ephesus in 431.

§ 7. At length the Council of Chalcedon met, 8th Oct.-1st Nov., 451.

At the first session, 8th Oct., the Roman legates presided: and Paschasinus took occasion to remind the Synod that he held in his hand " the instructions of the Pope of the city of Rome which is the head of all the Churches " to the effect that Dioscorus should be excluded from the assembly.[3] But the Imperial Commissioners who " presided for the sake of order "[4] insisted that, if this were done, it must be after trial: and Dioscorus, with his accuser Eusebius of Dorylæum, appeared in the midst. Similarly, Theodoret, in the view of the Commissioners, ought to be admitted: for " the Pope had restored him to the episcopate and the Emperor had commanded that he should take part in the Council."[5] He was admitted. But his restoration came up again for further consideration later. The rest of the day was devoted to an interminable

---

[1] *Epp.* xc.-xciii. (*P.L.* liv. 932-42): Jaffé, Nos. 470-73.
[2] *Optaveram quidem.*
[3] Mansi vi. 563 sq.
[4] The Council to Leo: *Ep.* xcviii. § 1 (*P.L.* liv. 951 sq.).
[5] Mansi vi. 589 B.

recitation of the minutes of the Council of Ephesus in 449 and of the Synod of Constantinople in 448, till at last the case against Dioscorus was clear enough, and his deposition was pronounced.

At the second session, 10th Oct., the Council was invited to devote itself to " the establishment of the true Faith."[1] They proceeded to read the Creeds of Nicæa and Constantinople, the second letter of Cyril to Nestorius and his letter to John of Antioch, followed by the Tome of St. Leo. All were at one—Commissioners, Pope and Council—in ignoring Cyril's third letter to Nestorius, the letter with the anathematisms. A minority was quick to notice this omission. Others, indeed, acclaimed the Tome, crying, "Peter hath spoken through Leo,"[2] meaning that Leo had brought out the true sense of Peter's confession; and others again, " Leo and Cyril have taught alike." But these found a difficulty with certain passages of the Tome, in which it appeared to them to approximate to Nestorianism. A demand was made for a few days wherein to compare the letter of Leo with the third letter of Cyril to Nestorius. The bishops pretended not to hear. But the Commissioners granted a five days' adjournment; and appointed a committee to consider and report.[3]

In the meanwhile, at a third session, 13th Oct., the Council took up, for ecclesiastical decision, the case of Dioscorus; for, at the end of the previous session, a few had requested consideration for him, though in vain. The Commissioners were not present.

[1] *Ib*. 952 C.   [2] *Ib*. 972 A, B.
[3] *Ib*. 973 D.

They had said their say, so far as Dioscorus was concerned. His affair was left to the Council, with Paschasinus, the papal legate, presiding.[1] Deputations were sent to summon Dioscorus; but he refused to come. So they proceeded against him for contumacy, the legates first summing up his misdeeds and pronouncing sentence. " Dioscorus," they declared, " has been guilty of many offences. He ignored the sentence of Flavian against Eutyches. He received Eutyches into communion. He refused to let the letter (sc. the Tome) of Leo be read. He dared to excommunicate Leo. And he has refused our repeated citations. Leo therefore, by us and by the present holy Synod, together with St. Peter, who is the rock of the Church and the basis of right Faith, deprives him of his episcopal dignity." A sonorous preface to a sentence which was not that of the Pope alone; for the legate continues, " Now therefore the Synod will vote in accordance with the canons."[2] And this the bishops in turn proceeded to do. One " agrees in all points with the Apostolic See." A second " subjects Dioscorus to ecclesiastical sentence, even as Leo and Anatolius [of Constantinople] have done." Others " judge "; " decide "; " give sentence." The sentence was thus not Leo's simply; but that of the Pope made its own by the Council. And so it is described in various reports; and in the synodical letter to Valentinian and Marcian and to Pulcheria. " Dioscorus has been stripped of his episcopate by the Œcumenical Council."[3]

[1] Mansi vi. 985 A.   [2] *Ib.* 1048 B.   [3] *Ib.* 1099 C.

§ 8. Dioscorus thus got rid of, the Council at its fourth session, 17th Oct., returned to the question of the Faith. The Imperial Commissioners presided once more; and, after having the minutes of the first two sessions read over, they requested the Council to express its mind concerning the Faith. In answer, Paschasinus on behalf of the legates referred to " The rule of faith as contained in the Creed of Nicæa, confirmed by the Council of Constantinople, expounded at Ephesus under Cyril, and set forth in the letter of Pope Leo when he condemned the heresy of Nestorius and Eutyches."[1] This statement the bishops received with shouts of assent. Thereupon, the Commissioners bade them one by one to declare if they considered " the expositions " of Nicæa and Constantinople " to be in accordance with the letter of the most reverend archbishop Leo." The meaning to be put upon the phrase is clear from their replies. " The letter of Leo," began Anatolius of Constantinople, " is in harmony with the Creed as well as with what was done at Ephesus under Cyril." " It is plain," said the legates themselves, " that the Faith of Leo is in harmony with the Creed, and with the Ephesian definitions, and therefore his letter is of the same sense as the Creed."[2] It is well to note this language of the papal representatives. So far from attributing to the papal letter any final and independent authority of its own, they declare that the Tome is to be accepted as being in accordance with the Creed and the subsequent doctrinal decisions of the episcopate. And the bishops accepted it, one

[1] Mansi vii. 9 A, B.   [2] *Ib.* 12 A.

by one, on this ground and no other. " It agrees ": or " Leo is shown to have accepted the Nicene Faith, as did Cyril." True, the bishops had many of them signed the Tome at an earlier stage: but the point is that they did not merely accept it on the authority of the Pope, as if that were all. They tested, approved and so raised it to the level of an Œcumenical standard of the Faith, precisely as the letter of Cyril to Nestorius had been examined, authenticated and raised to that rank, *after* it had received the approval of Pope Cœlestine. On the Vaticanist principle " that the definitions of the Roman Pontiff are irreformable of themselves, and not because of the consent of the Church,"[1] it was *de fide* from the date of its publication, 13th June, 449; but the Council did not treat it so. They examined it, and made it *de fide* on 17th Oct., 451.

We pass on to the eighth session, of 26th Oct., at which took place the rehabilitation of Theodoret. He had been deposed at the *Latrocinium*, recalled from exile by the Emperor, and admitted to the Council at its first session. But his final restoration was the act not of the Pope but of the Synod.[2]

§ 9. We now proceed to the sixteenth session, of 1st Nov., when the twenty-eighth canon,[3] which created a Patriarchate for the see of Constantinople, was met with determined opposition by the Roman legates. The canon runs as follows: " As in all things we follow the ordinances of the holy fathers, and know the canon,

[1] *Const. dogm. I de eccl. Christi*, § 4 (Mirbt⁴, No. 606, p. 466, ll. 1-2).

[2] See E. Denny, *Papalism*, §§ 397-401.

[3] Mirbt⁴, No. 180: *Doc. Ch. Hist.* ii., No. 215.

recently read, of the hundred and fifty bishops,[1] so do we decree the same in regard to the privileges of the most holy see of Constantinople, *i.e.* New Rome. Rightly have the fathers conceded to the see of Old Rome its privileges on account of its character as the Imperial City; and, moved by the same considerations, the hundred and fifty bishops have awarded the like privileges to the most holy see of New Rome, judging with good reason that the City which is honoured by the Imperial Power and the Senate, and enjoys the same privileges as the ancient Imperial City, should also in its ecclesiastical relations be exalted and hold the second place after that. And we decree that, for the dioceses of Pontus, Asia and Thrace, only the metropolitans but, in those of the neighbourhoods of the dioceses named which are inhabited by barbarians, also the (ordinary) bishops, shall be consecrated from the holy see of Constantinople; while naturally each metropolitan in the dioceses named shall in union with the bishops of the eparchy (province) consecrate the new bishops of those dioceses, as it is ordered in the holy canons. The metropolitans of the dioceses named shall, however, as has been said, be consecrated by the archbishop of Constantinople, after their election has been first unanimously agreed upon in the customary manner, and the election has been made known to the bishop of Constantinople."[2]

In practice, the canon made no innovation. It merely gave recognition to an existing state of affairs. It kept the Nicene rules about " ancient customs "

[1] CP. 3: A.D. 381.　　　　[2] Hefele, *Councils*, iii. 411 sq.

in spirit; but broke them in the letter. But it gave
great offence to the Roman legates; for, among other
things, it ascribed the pre-eminence of the Roman See
to the civil dignity of the city—an ascription which,
historically, was only part of the truth. The legates
now called attention to what had been done in the
absence of the Commissioners and of themselves, and
produced their instructions from Pope Leo. He had
enjoined them " to guard the ordinances of the Fathers
and the dignity of his own person " against possible
" usurpations on the part of those who might rely on
the splendour of their sees ";[1] and, as the synod had
ignored " the decisions of the three hundred and
eighteen at Nicæa " in favour of " the hundred and
fifty at Constantinople,"[2] the legates sought permission
of the Commissioners to refer to the Nicene authority.
Permission was given; and Paschasinus read out the
version of the sixth canon of Nicæa, then current in
Italy and Sicily, beginning: " The Roman church hath
always had the primacy; therefore let Egypt also have
it (sc. within the Egyptian limits), so that the bishop of
Alexandria should have authority over all, since this
is also customary for the Roman bishop; and similarly
let him who is appointed bishop in Antioch; and, in
the other provinces, let the churches of the larger
cities have the first place."[3] " Primacy " is here
used clearly of patriarchal jurisdiction: for what Rome
had in her region, Alexandria was to have in hers.
There could be no question of papalism; but, for all

---

[1] Mansi vii. 444 A.   [2] Ib. 441 D, E.
[3] Ib. 444: Mirbt[4], No. 111, n. 2.

that, the version of Paschasinus was immediately put out of court. The secretary of the Council confronted it with the original Greek of the Nicene canon; where, of course, no mention of any Roman primacy occurs; and he next read out the first three canons of " the hundred and fifty at Constantinople,"[1] which formed the basis of the legislation now in hand. The Council consented.[2] The Commissioners then gave their decision[3] in favour of the twenty-eighth canon. In vain the legates entered a final protest, and said that they could not sit by and see " the Apostolic see humiliated in our presence."[4] " Our sentence," replied the Commissioners, " has been approved by the whole synod."

§ 10. So ended the Council of Chalcedon. To secure the papal assent they sent a synodical letter to Leo.[5] Here, after the manner of Jacob in dealing with Esau, they first appease him not with presents but with honorific titles, and then delicately approach the point. They acknowledge him, § 1, as " the interpreter of Peter," as " the head " of their synod; as having entertained them, by his Tome, to nothing less than " a spiritual banquet "; and, § 2, as " the divinely-appointed guardian of the Vine," for excommunicating whom Dioscorus had been deposed. They then proceed to inform him, § 4, that they have lent their authority to a custom of long standing and have ordained that the Church of Constantinople should consecrate metropolitans for the dioceses of Asia,

[1] *Ib*. 445. [2] *Ib*. 453 A.
[3] *Ib*. 452 sq. [4] *Ib*. 453 C.
[5] Leo, *Ep*. xcviii. (*P.L.* liv. 951-60).

Pontus and Thrace, not so much with a view to the
advantage of Constantinople as for the peace of metro-
political sees in those regions, so often disturbed at
the elections of their bishops. They have also confirmed the canon which gave rank to the bishop of
Constantinople next after Leo's own See; and are
confident of the Pope's goodwill in this matter. His
legates, it is true, " opposed our project; but doubtless
from a desire that your Holiness might have the honour
of making the suggestion yourself ! At any rate, it
was the wish of the Emperor, the Senate and the
entire city. It would have been ungracious to do
otherwise than acquiesce ! "

A letter in this tone was too clever by half for a
plain man like Leo; and, as if anticipating the bad
impression that it would make, both Marcian and
Anatolius thought well to supplement it. Their cue
was to presume that the legates of Leo did not really
know his mind, and so to try to detach him from their
proceedings. " They did their level best," wrote the
Emperor, 18th Dec., 451, " to prevent the synod from
enacting anything concerning this venerable Church ";[1]
while Anatolius added that Leo's legates " not knowing
his real mind disturbed the synod and grossly insulted
both me and the church of Constantinople."[2] But
the Pope knew well that his representatives had both
understood his wishes and had loyally carried them
out. He was not to be propitiated. He determined to
get rid of the obnoxious legislation, and had reasons

[1] Leo, *Ep*. c. § 3 (*P.L.* liv. 972 A).
[2] *Ib*. ci. (*P.L.* liv. 984 A).

against it—one powerful, but unworthy of him: the others sound. Thus, in the elevation of Constantinople to the second Patriarchate, he feared a rival to his own; and this was a weighty, though hardly a worthy, reason for opposition. Next, he foresaw that this second Patriarch in Christendom would run the risk of becoming a Pope dependent upon the Court, and feared the subjection of the Church to the State. True, the State was, for the moment, Pulcheria; but, after that Orthodox Empress, there might well ensue an epoch of Byzantinism unalloyed. Further, the Pope may well have had fears for the unity of Christendom. It was now fairly safe under the ancient régime of the whole episcopate with the Pope for its president; but, with the Greek episcopate looking to a chief of its own at Constantinople, and that chief enjoying his pre-eminence and his jurisdiction not as bishop of an Apostolic see but simply as bishop of the Imperial city, there was only too clear a prospect of schism ahead. Once again, if the civil pre-eminence of a city was to entitle its bishop forthwith to supreme ecclesiastical authority, then Rome itself and Leo would have to give place to the archbishop of Ravenna, the capital of Valentinian III. Solid reasons all, for resistance on Leo's part; but just the very reasons which he could not publicly avow. His legates, indeed, had intimated that he might ground his refusal of assent either upon the injury done to his own see or upon the Nicene canons. He was wise enough to decline the former suggestion; but to stake all, as he did, upon the permanence of the Nicene arrangements

and the inviolability of Nicene canons as such was to
adopt a position which, whatever it might promise in
dealing with Easterns, soon proved to be quite untenable.

Such, however, was the line that he chose when,
in letters[1] of 22nd May, 452, he replied to the Eastern
Sovereigns and to Anatolius. With much to say about
" the ambition " and " the intemperate cupidity " of
the Patriarch of Constantinople—which reminds us
of Popes less single-minded than Leo—he goes back
to the irregularities in the ecclesiastical career of Anatolius. He had been consecrated by Dioscorus, upon
the unjust deposition of Flavian; and, while Domnus
was still in legal possession of Antioch, he had consecrated Maximus to that dignity. Anatolius therefore,
as Leo reminds the Emperor, " ought to reflect that
I have treated him with lenity rather than justice in
admitting his irregular ordination[2] and in winking at
his uncanonical promotion of Maximus;[3] and this
advice the Pope repeats to Anatolius himself.[4] " A
little of his predecessor Flavian's modesty," Leo tells
Pulcheria, " is what he most needs ":[5] so let him not
presume on a concession wrung from his brethren.
It can avail nothing against the canons, especially
those of Nicæa: for the decrees of that Council, he
bids Anatolius remember, are both " inviolable "[6]
and " eternal."[7] So much for the personal element
behind the legislation The Pope then turns to the
political and the ecclesiastical. " Of course," he

---

[1] *Ep.* civ.-cvi. (*P.L.* liv. 991-1010): Jaffé, Nos. 481-483.
[2] *Ep.* civ. § 2.   [3] *Ib.* § 5.   [4] *Ep.* cvi.
[5] *Ep.* cv. § 3.   [6] *Ep.* cvi. § 2.   [7] *Ib.* § 4.

observes to Marcian, " Constantinople has its privileges; but they are purely secular. It is an Imperial city. It can never become an Apostolic see. And he loses his own who covets more than his due."[1] Neither the rights of Alexandria and Antioch, both Petrine sees, nor the primacy of so many metropolitans should be so lightly sacrificed. With our eye upon the ambition of Leo and several of his successors, pursued no less than that of Anatolius at the expense of other sees, and upon the losses to the papacy consequent upon it, we cannot but note an irony in reading of Leo as champion of the rights of other prelates. But this was the only line open to him: to get the obnoxious canon invalidated by an appeal to the authority of Nicæa. " Let me urge it upon your Holiness," he wrote, 21st March, 453, to the bishops who had been present at Chalcedon,[2] " that the rights of churches must remain just as they were ordained by the three hundred and eighteen divinely inspired fathers." He does not, it will be observed, appeal to the principles of papalism[3] in order to get the canon cancelled, as if it set up a second Pope at Constantinople and so sinned against the Divine Constitution of the Church. He simply appeals to Eastern veneration for the Council of Nicæa, and in such terms as to enlist upon his side the jealousy which Alexandria and Antioch might be expected to feel against " sixty years' "[4] successful

---

[1] *Ep*. civ. § 3.
[2] *Omnem quidem fraternitatem* (*Ep*. cxiv. § 2): Jaffé, No. 490.
[3] E. Denny, *Papalism*, § 442.
[4] *Ep*. cv. § 2.

encroachment by an upstart rival. The appeal fell on deaf ears.

But the quarrel was embarrassing to the Government, and so had to be composed. On the one hand, the Tome of Leo was widely resented, and the Government had to bring troops into the field to get the doctrinal decisions of the Council obeyed. On the other hand, its administrative arrangements were disallowed by the Pope. A *rapprochement* of some sort became imperative. At last, in reply to an appeal of 15th Feb., 453, from the Emperor,[1] Leo on his part was induced to declare, 21st March, that so far as the Faith was concerned he expressly approved of the Council of Chalcedon,[2] without being required[3] to desist from his protest in favour of the canons of Nicæa. Anatolius, in his turn, was encouraged to assert the rank and the jurisdiction lately conferred upon him, while the need for Leo's assent was ignored. It was a victory for the Faith: but a defeat for the papal claim to a primacy of jurisdiction. " In vain did Pope Leo protest; the nominal concessions granted to him in no way stopped the progress of an ecclesiastical centralisation around the capital and its archbishop."[4]

§ 11. The Petrine theory, as finally put into shape by Leo, was, no doubt, held in good faith, and as the only guarantee of unity. " He wished to prevent the establishment in the East of a unity of which the bishop of Constantinople would be the chief, and

---

[1] Leo, *Ep.* cx. (*P.L.* liv. 1017-20).
[2] *Ep.* cxiv. § 1.   [3] *Ib.* § 2.
[4] Duchesne, *The Churches Separate from Rome*, 130.

which would be opposed to the unity of the West by isolating itself therefrom. He discerned a danger that threatened the unity of the Church, such as the sovereign primacy of the Apostolic See could alone resist."[1] The theory has undergone little modification since Leo's day, except in one point. " It is not now maintained that the Pope, as the successor of St. Peter, is the necessary channel of all episcopal jurisdiction, and that the bishops receive the powers of their ministry through him. . . . According to the doctrine now usually taught by Roman Catholic theologians, while the mission and jurisdiction of the bishops are inherent in their office and their sees, and are received and possessed by them as a matter of divine right bestowed by our Lord Himself, the episcopate forms one body with the Pope, not as an independent body apart from him; and consequently the bishops have no power to exercise the mission and jurisdiction which they receive from our Lord unless they are in external communion with the Pope."[2] A happy adjustment: but all the other elements of the Leonine theory have remained and are to be found set forth by the Vatican Council.[3] The Council affirms (1) " the institution of the primacy in blessed Peter " and " a primacy not of honour only but of true and proper jurisdiction ";[4] (2) " the perpetuity of the primacy of blessed Peter in the Roman pontiffs "[5]—" his successors, in whom he

---

[1] Batiffol, *Le siège apostolique*, 577 sq.
[2] D. Stone, *The Christian Church*, 171.
[3] Mirbt[4], No. 606.
[4] *Const. dogm. de Eccl.* I. § 1: *ib.*, p. 462, l. 22.
[5] *Ib.* § 2, p. 462, ll. 41-3.

lives and presides and judges to this day ";[1] and (3) " the
power and nature of the primacy of the Roman pontiff "[2]
to be " the supreme power of governing the Universal
Church."[3] But what are the grounds on which these
claims rest ?

(1) The primacy of Peter is based by the Council
on two of the Petrine texts: Matt. xvi. 16-19 and
John xxi. 15-17; the third, Luke xxii. 32, is taken as
dealing not with jurisdiction but with infallibility,
and does not concern us here. Now there can be no
doubt that Peter enjoyed a primacy of leadership
among the other Apostles. The New Testament
evidence for it is well set out by Dr. C. H. Turner.[4]
But we do not find any " unanimous consent of the
Fathers "[5] in favour of one, and only one, interpretation
of the Petrine texts. " The ' Rock ' is sometimes
interpreted of St. Peter, sometimes of our Lord, sometimes of the true faith in Christ. . . . The gift of the
keys, the promise to bind and loose, are regarded as
the common possession of the Apostles by, among
others, Origen, St. Ambrose and St. Augustine. Nor
is there better patristic authority for any one interpretation of the other two passages. Of John xxi. 15-17
Augustine says that this charge was given by our Lord

---

[1] *Const. dogm. de Eccl.* I. § 2, Mirbt[4], No. 606, p. 462, ll. 33
and 34: where the Vatican Council attributes to the Council of
Ephesus words which were only those of Philip, the papal
legate: see above c. viii. § 3.

[2] *Ib.*, p. 463, l. 1.   [3] *Ib.*, p. 463, l. 30: and p.464, l. 5.

[4] *Catholic and Apostolic*, pp. 148-214.

[5] Creed of Pope Pius IV. (1564), Mirbt[4], No. 480: note
" juxta " of this Creed is changed by the Vatican Council
to " non contra ": *ib.*, No. 605, p. 457, l. 37.

to all the Apostles and that the particular address to
St. Peter was because he was the first in order of the
Apostolic band; and St. Cyril of Alexandria regards
it not as a gift of or allusion to any special position
among the Apostles, but as a renewal of St. Peter's
office as an Apostle, as a mark that his sin in denying
our Lord had been forgiven."[1] We must therefore
reject the claim to a primacy of jurisdiction, so far as
it depends for its support on the evidence of the New
Testament and the Fathers.

(2) Neither can the perpetuation of a primacy of
this sort in Peter and his successors be sustained.
For, if the earliest episcopal lists of the Roman church
and the Canon of the Mass preserve, as they do, its
older tradition, then the Apostles Peter and Paul stand
in a class by themselves, and Linus was by their appointment the first bishop of Rome. Peter, that is, was never
bishop of Rome. He had no successors in that see.
And no bishop of Rome succeeded to his prerogatives.

(3) Finally, as to the nature of the Roman primacy,
it was a primacy of leadership: more than a primacy of
honour, though less than a primacy of jurisdiction:
and the bishop of Rome, as occupant of the first
Apostolic See in Christendom, derives from St. Peter
and St. Paul, the twin founders, in the sense of organ-
izers, of the church in Rome, that pre-eminence which
has been accorded to him everywhere, always and by
all, and is still generally recognized as his.

[1] D. Stone, *The Christian Church*, 201 sq.; with references,
which are given more fully by him in *The Church Quarterly
Review* for January, 1897.

INDEX

Acacius, bishop of Constantinople, 78

Ad limina Apostolorum, 22

Adoptianism, 40

Africa, church of, 81 *sqq.*, 124

Alypius, bishop of Tagaste, 100

Ambrose, bishop of Milan, 66 *sqq.*, 70 *n.*, 154

Anastasius, Pope, 76

Anatolius, archbishop of Constantinople, 140 *sqq.*, 150 *sqq.*

Antioch:
  Church of, 61, 64 *sq.*
  Councils of, 40 *sq.*, 47, 50, 63

Antony, bishop of Fussala, 96 *sq.*

Apostle-founder, theory of the, 20 *sqq.*, 71

Apiarius, 97 *sqq.*, 126

Appeals to Rome, 85 *sq.*, 97 *sq.*, 113, 125 *sq.*, 131, 134 *sqq.*

Aquileia:
  Church of, 76
  Council of, 66

Arianism, 45 *sqq.*

Ariminum, Council of, 54

Arles:
  Councils of, 43, 53
  See of, 88, 124 *sqq.*

Athanasius, bishop of Alexandria, 47 *sq.*, 55, 94

Atticus, bishop of Constantinople, 102

Augustine, bishop of Hippo, 81, 84, 87, 96 *sq.*, 101, 154

Aurelian, Emperor, 41

Aurelius, bishop of Carthage, 89, 97, 100 *sq.*

Basil, archbishop of Cæsarea in Cappadocia, 60 *sqq.*

Basilides, a Spanish bishop, 29 *sq.*

Bellarmine, 83

Benedict XIV, Pope, 82 *sq.*

Boniface, Pope, 77, 91, 96

Cæcilian, bishop of Carthage, 42 *sq.*, 99, 102

Cæsaropapism, 45 *sq.*, 53

Caius the presbyter, 15

Callistus, Pope, 22, 36

Canon of the Mass, The, 18, 136, 155

Carthage, Councils of, 25, 32 *sqq.*, 43 n., 81 *sqq.*, 86, 98, 100, 124

Cathedra Petri, The, 26 *sqq.*, 35, 71

Celidonius, bishop of Besançon, 125 *sq.*

Chalcedon, Council of, 129

Chrysostom, 77, 85 *sqq.*

Church and State, 45, 60, 126 *sqq.*, 149

Clement of Rome, 11, 16 *sqq.*
  first epistle of, 11 *sq.*, 21 *sq.*

Clementine Romances, The, 21

Cœlestine, Pope, 95 *sqq.*, 103 *sqq.*

Constantine, Emperor, 42 *sqq.*

Constantinople:
  Councils of, 12, 62 *sqq.*, 68, 114, 131, 141, 145
  See of, 144 *sqq.*, 151

Constantius II, Emperor, 42, 47 *sqq.*

Convenire ad, meaning of, 15

Cornelius, Pope, 29 n., 31

Creeds:
  African, 32
  Roman, 48

Creeds:
"The Blasphemy" of Sirmium, 54
of Ulphilas, 64 n.
Cunctos populos, 63
Cursus honorum, The, 25 n.
Cyprian, bishop of Carthage, 23 *sqq.*, 71, 95
Cyril, archbishop of Alexandria, 40, 102, 106 *sqq.*, 140, 155

Damasus, Pope, 56 *sqq.*, 93, 125
Decentius, bishop of Eugubium, 80
D e c r e t u m Gelasianum (so-called) of Damasus, 69 *sqq.*
Dionysius, bishop of Corinth, 12 *sqq.*
Dionysius, bishop of Alexandria, 36 *sqq.*
Dionysius, Pope, 38 *sqq.*
Dioscorus, archbishop of Alexandria, 130 *sqq.*, 140 *sqq.*
Donatism, 42 *sqq.*
Donatists, 29 *sq.*, 98

Ecclesiæ transmarinæ, 76, 98
Ephesus, Councils of:
(431), 106 *sqq.*, 140
(449), 133 *sqq.*, 141
Epiphanius, 16
Episcopal lists, 16 *sq.*, 136, 155
Et hoc Gloriæ Vestræ, 57
Eudoxia, Empress (wife of Arcadius), 85
Eudoxia, Empress (wife of Valentinian III), 138
Eusebius, bishop of Cæsarea, 16
Eusebius, bishop of Dorylæum, 131, 135, 140
Eusebius, bishop of (1) Nicomedia, (2) Constantinople, 47
Eusebius, bishop of Vercelli, 53
Eutyches, 123, 130 *sqq.*
Exuperius, bishop of Toulouse, 78 *sq.*

Faustinus, papal legate, 96 *sq.*, 101 *sqq.*

Filial subordination, The, 39
Firmilian, bishop of Cæsarea in Cappadocia, 35 *sq.*
Flavian, archbishop of Constantinople, 130 *sqq.*
Flavian, bishop of Antioch, 65 *sqq.*, 76, 94
Forged Decretals, The, 49, 128 n.
Formula of Reunion, The, 113, 115, 129

Galla Placidia, Empress, 117, 138
Germanus, bishop of Auxerre, 125
Gratian, Emperor, 57 *sqq.*, 67, 77, 127
Gregory of Nazianzus, bishop of Constantinople, 62 *sqq.*

ἡγεμονία and ἀρχή, 137
Hegesippus, 16
Hilary, archbishop of Arles, 124 sqq., 138
Hilary, bishop of Poitiers, 53
Hilary, Pope, 133 *sq.*
Himerius, bishop of Tarragona, 73 *sq.*
Hippolytus, 17, 22, 71
Honorius, Emperor, 77, 90
Hormisdas, Pope, 65
Hosius, bishop of Cordova, 45 *sq.*

Ignatius to the Romans, Epistle of, 12 *sq.*
Illyricum, Papal Vicariate of, 63, 67 *sq.*, 75 *sqq.*, 88, 91 *sqq.*, 95, 114 *sqq.*, 121 *sq.*
Innocent I, Pope, 77 *sqq.*, 89 *sq.*
Innocent X, Pope, 136
Irenæus, 14 *sqq.*, 20 *sqq.*

John, bishop of Antioch, 112 *sqq.*
John the Apostle, St., 11, 20
Jubaianus, a bishop of Mauretania, 34
Julian, bishop of Cos, 133, 140

Julius, Pope, 40, 47 *sqq.*
Jurisdiction:
> Episcopal and papal, 153
> Papal primacy of, 11, 135

Latrocinium, The, 133, 144
Legatus a latere, 104
Leo I, Pope, 83, 95, 112, 116 *sqq.*
Leo XIII, Pope, 82
Liberian Catalogue, The, 17
Liberius, Pope, 17, 53 *sqq.*
Linus, 16 *sqq.*, 155

Marcian, bishop of Arles, 30, 44
Marcian, Emperor, 139 *sqq.*
Marcion, 34
Martialis, a Spanish bishop, 29 *sq.*
Maximian, archbishop of Constantinople, 111
Meletius, bishop of Antioch, 61 *sqq.*
Milan, 44, 55, 76
> Councils of, 53, 66 *sq.*
Milevum, Council of, 81 *sqq.*
Miltiades, Pope, 43 *sq.*
Monarchical government of the Church, 82, 95, 137
Monophysites, 129 *sq.*

Nestorius, archbishop of Constantinople, 106 *sqq.*
Nicæa, Council of, 41 *sq.*, 45 *sq.*, 76, 79, 86, 93, 100 *sqq.*, 149 *sqq.*
Non-Roman rite of the West, 80
Novatianists, 30

[*Occidentalis*] *ecclesiæ præsidens*, 87
Optatus, 27
Ordinariorum Sententiæ, 58 *sq.*
Origen, 76, 154

Paschasinus, bishop of Lilybæum, 139 *sqq.*
Paul of Samosata, 40 *sqq.*
Paulinus, bishop at Antioch, 61 *sq.*
Pelagianism, 81 *sqq.*

Perigenes, bishop of Corinth, 91 *sq.*
Peter and Paul, 14 *sqq.*, 21, 69, 113, 122, 136, 155
Peter Chrysologus, archbishop of Ravenna, 123, 131
Peter in N.T., 154
Peter in Peter's see, 75, 92, 118, 122
Petrine hierarchy, Theory of a, 69 *sqq.*, 95, 151
Petrine Texts, The, 22, 27, 70 *sq.*, 87, 93, 118 *sq.*, 133, 154
Petrine theory, The, 152 *sqq.*
Philip, papal legate, 96 *sq.*, 107, 109 *sq.*
φύσις and ὑπόστασις, 129 *sq.*
Pius VII, Pope, 53
Plenitudo potestatis, 123
Polycarp, 21
Pompey, bishop of Sabrata, 33
Pope and episcopate, Relation of, 153
Potestas jurisdictionis, 82
" Primacy of honour," 11, 65, 155
" Primacy of jurisdiction," 11, 70 n., 155
Proclus, archbishop of Constantinople, 114 *sq.*
Pulcheria, Empress, 139 *sqq.*

Quintus, a bishop of Mauretania, 33

Ravenna, 77, 97, 131, 149
Ravennius, archbishop of Arles, 129
Re-baptism, 32 *sqq.*
Relatio and *Rescriptum*, 74 *n.*
Roma locuta est : causa finita est, 84
Rome and Alexandria, relations of, 38 *sqq.*, 49, 94, 107 *sqq.*, 130
Rome:
> Church of, 11 *sqq.*, 14 n., 18
> Councils of, 43, 48, 57 63, 68 *sq.*, 106, 137

Rome:
    Episcopate of, 16 *sqq.*, 136, 155
    See of, 20 *sqq.*, 26, 35, 70, 135 *sq,*, 155
Rufinus of Aquileia, 76

Sabellianism, 39
Sardica:
    Canons of, 51 *sqq.*, 79, 99 *sq.*, 137 *sq.*
    Council of, 46 *sqq.*, 125 *sq.*
Satis cognitum, The, 82 n.
Simplicianus, bishop of Milan, 76
Siricius, Pope, 73 *sqq.*
Sirmium, Council of, 54
Sixtus II, Pope, 38, 40
Sixtus III, Pope, 112 *sqq.*
Stephen, Pope, 22 *sqq.*, 29 *sqq.*, 71
Suburbicarian churches, 75 *sq.*
Sylvester, Pope, 43, 46
Symmachus, Pope, 18
Synodical government, 124, 126

Tertullian, 15 n., 20 *sq.*, 36
Theodoret, bishop of Cyrrhus, 135 *sq.*, 140, 144
Theodosius I, Emperor, 63 *sqq.*, 77
Theodosius II, Emperor, 91, 107, 114, 130 *sqq.*

Theophilus, bishop of Alexandria, 76, 86
Thesaurus Græcorum Patrum, 128 n.
Thomas Aquinas, 82 n., 83, 128 n.
Tome of St. Leo, The, 132, 136, 143 *sq.*
Tu es Petrus, 24 *sqq.*, 36 *sq.*
Turribius, bishop of Astorga, 123
Tyre, Council of, 47, 50

Ulphilas, bishop of the Goths, 64
Ultra-Cyrillines, 129 *sqq.*
" Unanimous Consent of the Fathers, The," 154

Valens, Emperor, 60
Valentinian I, Emperor, 55
Valentinian III, Emperor, 117, 127 *sq.*, 131, 138 *sq.*
Vatican Council, 11, 111, 144, 153 *sqq.*
Venerius, bishop of Milan, 86
Vicar of Christ, 120 *sq.*
Victor, Pope, 18, 22
Victricius, bishop of Rouen, 78 *sq.*

Zenobia, Queen of Palmyra, 41
Zosimus, Pope, 87 *sqq.*, 97 *sqq.*